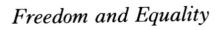

Freedom and Equality

Keith Dixon

Freedom and Equality

THE MORAL BASIS OF
DEMOCRATIC SOCIALISM

ROUTLEDGE & KEGAN PAUL
London, Boston and Henley

For young socialists

First published in 1986
by Routledge & Kegan Paul plc
14 Leicester Square, London WC2H 7PH, England
9 Park Street, Boston, Mass. 02108, USA and
Broadway House, Newtown Road,
Henley on Thames, Oxon RG9 1EN, England
Set in Imprint 11/13 Linotron 202
by Inforum Ltd, Portsmouth
and printed in Great Britain
by T J Press (Padstow) Ltd
Padstow, Cornwall

Library of Congress Cataloging in Publication Data

Dixon, Keith.
Freedom and equality.

Bibliography: p.
Includes index.
1. Liberty.   2. Equality.   3. Socialism.   I. Title.
JC585.D49 1986   320'.01'1   85–14539

ISBN 0–7102–0643–7

Contents

Contents

Acknowledgments

My thanks are due to Simon Fraser University for granting me sabbatical leave and to Southampton University Sociology and Social Administration Department for granting me Visiting Fellow status. Mrs Barbara Butler of SFU typed the manuscript with her usual meticulous attention to detail.

Introduction

'A society free from domination . . .
no more bowing and scraping, fawning and toadying;
no more fearful trembling no more high-and-mightiness;
no more masters, no more slaves.'
MICHAEL WALZER Spheres of Justice

This book is about the ideas of freedom and equality viewed as potentially realisable socialist ideals. I have made the somewhat optimistic assumption that there will be socialists around to realise them and that there is some point in addressing issues which presuppose that civilised forms of human organisation will continue to survive. This presupposition is clearly contingent upon nation-states being persuaded to abandon, whether unilaterally or otherwise, the manufacture and stockpiling of nuclear weapons. That issue, however, will not be addressed here.

I considered at one point entitling this essay 'The Principles of Social Democracy' since I am sceptical of political commitment to any 'ism'. Those who become enamoured of some general theory of society or some utopian vision often come to sacrifice present gains to future hopes and to ignore the legitimate wants and needs of individuals for the distant promise of collective harmony. I chose, however, to write of 'democratic socialism' rather than 'social democracy' for two reasons. First, as everyone knows, a political group in Britain has appropriated the label 'Social Democrat' in order to

I

distinguish itself from supposed Labour Party 'extremism'. The Social Democratic Party has very little to do, however, either with radical social change or the extension of democratic practices. It seeks, merely, to reformulate the 'politics of consensus' at a time when what is needed is radical change within a society ridden with inequalities of class, status and power and burdened by a tradition of excessive deference to established authority.

The second reason for my rejection of the term 'social democracy' is of far greater importance. Mr Roy Jenkins once remarked that 'socialism' was a word that he had ceased to use for many years. That observation was presumably intended to convey the impression that socialism was either empty of political content, hopelessly Utopian or simply politically undesirable. It cannot have escaped Mr Jenkins's notice however that the rank and file members of the Labour Party, many of whom worked for his re-election to Parliament, consistently use the word 'socialist' in a meaningful way. Were socialism merely a term connoting a blueprint for a new form of social and political organisation the degree of commitment to socialism on the part of active party workers and voters would be difficult to fathom. But, of course, the word is not primarily descriptive but symbolic. That is, the idea of socialism is what one might term 'rationally emotive'. It symbolises an aspiration towards the sort of society in which the evils of poverty, inequality, discrimination and arbitrary constraints upon personal liberty and autonomy are minimised. But socialism is not only forward-looking. Its meaning is indissolubly linked to the past history and struggles of the Labour movement. It is simultaneously the expression of the hopes, the successes, the frustrations and the sacrifices enjoyed and endured by generations of men and women who conceived of the possibility of a radically different, more generous and more open society than that which they currently inhabited. That is why the defections of Labour leaders and their subsequent derogation of the very political concepts which sustained their support is viewed as akin to betrayal.

Socialism is 'about equality', a prominent Labour Party politician once remarked. So it is. But it is not *just* about equality. Of course it is true that socialists have a commitment to the amelioration of the worst aspects of social hierarchy and perhaps to its eventual abolition. They aim at equality of respect and consideration as well as a more equal distribution of resources. And this aspect of socialist thought and action is of the greatest possible significance. Democratic socialists, however, are heirs to a tradition which values freedom both as a means to wider political ends and as an end-in-itself. That is, democratic socialists value freedom of thought, expression and association and ought to be committed to the doctrine that other things being equal individuals have the right to define and to pursue their own wants and satisfactions unhindered by authority or by the tyranny of orthodox opinion.

What consumes the urgent interest of most democratic socialists is how to achieve these aims politically by non-violent processes of persuasion. But there is the prior question of the coherence and compatibility of the twin ideals of freedom and equality. Notoriously, political systems which aim at implementing the 'summum bonum' through which all moral and political conflict and debate is magically resolved usually tend to the imposition upon their citizens of what Professor Maurice Cranston[1] has dubbed 'compulsive rational freedom'. That is, 'freedom' comes to be defined as 'justified coercion' in the interests of historical necessity or the future realisation of some mythical utopian society.

To stress only the possible incompatibility, however, between the ideas of freedom and equality is not to tell the whole story. Inequalities themselves are a form of constraint. If I am denied access to education, for example, by virtue of my class origins, my sex, or the colour of my skin, my choices are thereby diminished. If I live my life continuously subject

3

to hierarchical authority I am denied a sense of personal autonomy and control. My wants and needs become subject to definition by others and hence my freedom is restricted.

How then are freedom and equality to be defined? Are these two ideals compatible or incompatible? Or can the question be resolved only at the particular and specific level? Are there any political implications in choosing between the supposed variety of definitions of freedom and equality? Can we provide what Professor John Rawls[2] has referred to as a 'lexical ordering' of these principles? Can we, that is, argue that political freedom has necessary priority over claims to equality in a 'nearly just' society? If so, in what sense and under what specific conditions?

In what follows I do not proffer analyses of freedom and equality which are peculiarly or necessarily socialist. Indeed, I hold that there are no such animals. My analysis constitutes *the* meaning of the concepts. I do not, of course, believe that my view of freedom and equality is sacrosanct – far from it. Political ideas are always contestable by others of a different persuasion. What I wish to argue is that these ideas are definitive of democratic socialism only in the sense that both individual freedom and equality are moral imperatives of the highest order. In a just, socialist society one must strive to optimise application of both principles but this does not necessarily imply that one can aim for the total realisation of both ideals in political practice.

The ideas of freedom and equality are, it is argued, insufficient to exhaust the concept of democratic socialism. The word 'fraternity' (which I shall continue to use despite its supposedly 'sexist' connotations) is one which has a deep-seated significance for the Labour movement. It incorporates an ideal of 'equality of respect' based upon the metaphor of human kinship. But it goes beyond this. 'Fraternity' is distinguishable from equality in that it asserts the desirability of adopting a certain set of attitudes towards others. Namely, that a socialist society ought not to be dominated by mere contractual obligations but rather than the basis of civil society rests upon civic cooperation. No matter how effective governments are in promoting the public good, it may be argued, the full realisation of that good is predicated upon trust and respect amongst citizens. The concept of fraternity in the socialist's vocabulary stands opposed to the welter of often conflicting political theories based upon the notion of a social contract. A democratic socialist society ideally connotes not merely a society governed by mutual agreements; it encourages mutual sympathy and uncoerced cooperation. Whether this is a necessary condition of socialism is, however, a moot point.

Now it may be objected at this stage that my sketch of the main principles of democratic socialism has excluded consideration of the ideas of those persons who, whilst retaining membership in democratic socialist parties, owe their inspiration and allegiance primarily to the writings of Marx, Engels, Lenin and Trotsky and their successors. This is intentional. The 'left wing' of the various democratic socialist parties – in which broad category I include myself – has often exhibited a largely sentimental attitude towards Marx and neo-Marxism. Marx and Engels were indeed amongst the first social theorists to observe and to systematise the facts of class conflict. Marx, in particular, was assiduous in compiling information upon the manifest and brutal oppression of the European working class. Both men, in spite of their disclaimers, issued fervent moral denunciations of nineteenth century capitalism. All this can be accepted. But what is readily overlooked or discounted by democratic socialists is that this combination of honest observation and moral anger was set in a particular theoretical context. Marx's historicism – his doctrine of the historical inevitability of communism – his debt to the obscure, metaphysical writings of Hegel and his contempt for ideas other than those underwritten by a politically conscious proletariat – 'false consciousness' – are all inimical to the principles of democratic socialism. Furthermore most contemporary self-confessed 'Marxists' often show a cavalier disregard for civil liberties. And, of course, whatever the potentialities of a Marxist analysis of society it has to be pointed out repeatedly that no existing Marxist state has anywhere or at any time demonstrated concern for the most elementary civil liberties of its citizens in comparison with the much despised 'bourgeois democracies' of the West. This of course does not entail that democratic socialist parties ought necessarily to prohibit 'Marxists' from joining their political organisations. What has to be remembered, however, is that many Marxist, Leninist or 'Trotskyist' factions or 'tendencies' are fundamentally opposed to democratic socialism. Their allegiance to their chosen party is transient, expedient and dishonest. And ultimately they seek to subvert its goals.

Be that as it may, it is also well documented that many European socialist parties have failed – whether through the perceived influence of 'external economic forces' or through apathy or presumed electoral advantage – to achieve radical transformations in the redistribution of wealth, prestige and power.

Radical transformations, however, cannot be undertaken lightly. There is too much at stake for the future of civil liberties, individual needs and public welfare to embark upon wholesale egalitarian measures, necessary as they are, without careful thought for the consequences for other prized values.

Both the Conservative right and the Marxist left seek to foster the view that democratic socialism is dead both intellectually and as practical politics. Ian Gilmour has written modestly that 'Conservatism has probably won the intellectual battle'[3] whilst Marxists look forward to the demise of democratic socialism as the 'internal contradictions of capitalism' necessarily reveal its fundamental irrelevance. Both views are mistaken. The former is wishful thinking; the latter pure superstition.

There has however recently re-emerged in political writing a relatively rare animal – the philosophical sophisticated defence of traditional conservatism. Perhaps the most influential of this new breed has been Roger Scruton's 'work of dogmatics' *The Meaning of Conservatism*.[4] Scruton argues that liberal and democratic socialist doctrines are over-intellectualised and abstract. Such doctrines, he argues, neglect the particular national and institutional setting in which political commitment is realised. Conservatism, he suggests, is a largely inarticulate, but still 'systematic and reasonable', political response. It is to be associated with 'faith in arrangements that are known and tried' and in the creation of an 'objective public realm' as an end in itself which is an expression of social order. Authority, hierarchy, allegiance, law and tradition are held to be self-justifying features of society – or rather, of particular societies since any abstract political concept needs to be interpreted in terms of its particular historical and national meaning. Scruton's analysis is far from being a bland defence of 'free-enterprise'. Indeed he argues that the concept of freedom (and especially economic freedom) 'cannot occupy a central place in conservative thinking'. 'Freedom', he writes, 'is comprehensible as a social goal only when subordinate to something else, to an organisation . . . which defines the individual aim.'[5]

In stark contrast to these arguments I shall seek to show that the ideas of freedom and equality are simultaneously politically realisable ends and distinguishable moral ideals. What democratic socialism fundamentally consists in is the attempt to optimise these ideals in practice. This process cannot issue in a utopian state since neither of these principles is realisable *in toto*. Socialists are not working towards a New Jerusalem but towards the best possible form of humanly organised and humanly recognisable society. Such a transformed society may well appear 'utopian' when contrasted with any existing society. But that is merely a sad reflection upon existing social arrangements. It is not a counter-argument in itself.

The criticism by cynics, blinkered social determinists and others that such moral ideals are inherently unattainable ignores the fact that moral criticism – independently of grosser economic and social causation – has played a significant role in the development of socialist thought and action. Socialists ought never to abandon their creative moral intelligence to the idiocies of social, economic or genetic determinisms from whatever source these arise. To abandon the possibility of striving towards ideals is thereby to render those ideas socially ineffective and is a capitulation either to irrational dogmatism or to the guardians of the status quo whose main interest lies in the continuance of the present deadening burden of hierarchy and class orthodoxy.

1 The idea of freedom

'To know one's chains for what they are is better than to deck them with flowers.'

ROUSSEAU

(i) A stark outline of freedom as absence of constraint

Poets, metaphysicians and theologians have all written about the idea of freedom. Freedom has been celebrated in verse, distorted in philosophy, and conjured with by apologists for half a dozen world religions. Hegel wrote of freedom, in prolix and obscure prose, that it is 'necessity transfigured'. Theologians have declared human freedom to be a mystery and a challenge whilst practising the rooting out of heretics with a vigour that was anything but mysterious. Existentialists have seen human freedom as a source of generalised human 'angst' – an anxiety-ridden sense of total responsibility which is perhaps more characteristic of neurotics than of the emotionally robust defenders of civil liberties down the ages. For the most part such writings have no direct relevance to politics except in so far as they have obscured the idea of freedom in flights of fancy expressed in intricate verbiage.

Fortunately, we do not have to be possessed of mystical powers or to have a command of esoteric terminology to understand what freedom is or more usually what it is *not*!

The fact of imprisonment, restrictive government legislation, the controls exercised by corporate bureaucracies and
the censorship of opinion are pretty familiar no matter what
society we are members of. Most of us, then, view freedom
'negatively' as the absence of these kinds of constraints – the
absence of constraints, that is, upon our wishes, desires,
wants and needs.[1] Of course we do not believe that the
exercise of freedom is always justified. Our moral and political evaluations depend upon particular contexts. Whether we
approve of 'government interference in the market place' or
are opposed to restrictions upon 'free collective bargaining' is
dependent upon the degree to which we feel that the freedom
granted to the few diminishes the freedom of the many or
whether we feel that certain freedoms may be sacrificed in the
interests of promoting social harmony, full employment,
equality of opportunity or some other perceived socially
desirable end.

Nevertheless the word 'freedom' is not, in common par-
lance, without strong emotional overtones. Every political
party or social movement seems to appropriate the word
'freedom' for its own propaganda purposes. The IRA fights
for 'freedom from British colonial rule'; Conservatives speak
of the virtues of 'the free market' or 'free enterprise' rather
than 'capitalism'. Attach the word 'free' to any political ban-
ner and you assure your supporters of the sanctity of your
cause – whether it is the freedom to withdraw labour or the
freedom to spend your 'unearned' income in whatever way
you choose. The freedoms of which we disapprove, however,
are often not described as such. Here we object not to 'freedom' but to 'licence' – a question-begging term which ought
to be expunged from the vocabulary of politics.

It may be thought that the conception of freedom as 'not to
be impeded in the realisation of one's wants by some kind of
constraint' is little more than a superficial dictionary definition. Surely, it may be asserted, socialism isn't primarily
concerned with encouraging people to do as they please?

What of notions of social and communal responsiblity which lie at the heart of what is, after all, 'a collectivist philosophy'.

I shall discuss these objections later in the section on conceptions of 'Positive freedom'. Meanwhile let me make two brief observations. First, if by 'collectivism' is meant that set of beliefs and practices through the operation of which democratically elected groups intervene to protect and promote the interests of the weak, the poor and the underprivileged then this is wholly consistent with the negative interpretation of the idea of freedom. State intervention, though clearly an interference with the liberty of some individuals or groups, may be directed towards enhancing the liberty and interests of others. One may ask or demand that some people sacrifice the right to do as they choose in order to promote the civil liberty or material interests of others. What is inconsistent with 'negative freedom' is the totalitarian doctrine that the social collectivity – nation, state or group – stands over and above the individuals who comprise it. Such a doctrine – 'social holism' – is the notion that the state or society has special attributes, needs and authority independent of its citizenry. Such mystical conceptions of the state are generally promoted in totalitarian societies by ruling groups who seek to suppress minority opinion. The 'general will' overides the 'will of all' or of the separate conflicting wills of diverse political interest groups and individuals.

This 'holist' view is propagated as ideology in the strictest sense of that much abused word. That is, a conception of the state or civil society is propagated and functions merely in order to justify and to defend the interest of the rulers. Such ideologies often make use of an 'organic metaphor' of society. Just as a living organism is more than the sum of its material parts so, it is asserted, is 'society'. Society is conceived of on the analogy of the human body in which the organs function harmoniously to contribute to the health of the whole. The very phrase 'the body-politic' imports such analogies. Here there are a number of built-in assumptions. First there is the implication of the necessity of hierarchy – after all the brain 'governs', controls and coordinates the functions of the body –; second, social conflict is treated as pathological – as evidence of 'ill-health' or 'social sickness' and political opposition is construed of as positively harmful. 'Excrescences' on the body-politic need to be excised by the surgical knife – a metaphor for political murder, arbitrary imprisonment and revolutionary excess. This form of 'collectivism' encourages and supports visions of successful tyranny or of a non-historical conflict free Utopia. There is in practice little to choose between them and certainly these conceptions of society are wholly antipathetic to democratic socialism and indeed any form of so-called 'pluralism' which acknowledges both the inevitability and desirability of divergence of opinion and interest.

There is a clear sense in which democratic socialism is concerned to enable people to do as they please without constraint – that is, with the development of personal autonomy. Of course one hopes for and would encourage the autonomous pursuit of other morally desirable ends – tolerance, generosity, sympathy, the development of one's talents, and so forth. But these other virtues must not be confused with the exercise of freedom of choice. Ultimately one must concede (reluctantly or otherwise) that individuals are the best judges of their interests and wants and have the right to pursue them – other things being equal. Upon what other basis could one finally recommend democratic politics?

What the negative conception of freedom allows for is the moral judgment that freedom, seen as absence of constraint, may be an end-in-itself 'uncontaminated' by other values. Of course freedom is only prima facie desirable and there are occasions upon which it may justifiably be sacrificed. Nevertheless in justifying constraint or interference with what people want to do the burden is always upon the potential constrainer to demonstrate that interference with liberty will lead to a manifest greater good. What constitutes that 'greater good' is, of course the stuff of moral and political debate.

I have deliberately presented the negative conception of freedom in the starkest possible way. But, of course, I have omitted consideration of some of the more profound objections to this interpretation. 'Negative freedom' has been described by a distinguished left-wing philosopher as 'counter-intuitive' and its defenders, such as myself, are said to exhibit a 'Maginot-line mentality' in their quest to defend the indefensible. For, it is argued, there are very serious conceptual difficulties which have been overlooked. What, for example, is to count as a constraint upon freedom? Do cultural, social and psychological factors operate as constraints or are we speaking merely of constraints upon freedom exercised by identifiable human agents? Can people's wants be regarded as basic? If so in what sense? For surely it is true that some people have only hazy conceptions of what is in their own interest? 'Wants' are, in any case, frequently manufactured by those seeking to exploit human desire for profit. And what of the link between freedom and rationality, freedom and self-mastery? Are socialists committed to the acceptance of 'immature' or 'frivolous' exercises of freedom? Could a society be truly called socialist if the majority of its citizens chose autonomously to spend the greater part of their time watching TV soap operas, swilling beer, playing bingo or engaging in the manifold activities of which puritan intellectuals so disapprove? My own answer to these questions may perhaps prove surprising. But before essaying further dogmatic assertions I need to address more closely the arguments of critics who believe that a richer, fuller, more morally 'positive' conception of freedom is available than that articulated here. Charles Taylor in an article 'What's wrong with negative liberty?'[2] argues that pretty much everything is wrong with it and that it is a naive and philistine view which is unworthy of general acceptance – let alone by those who place themselves on the political left.

(ii) Positive conceptions of freedom

Charles Taylor asserts that proponents of the negative idea of freedom 'seem prone to embrace the crudest versions of their theory'. He suggests that they do so because their polemical intent is to fight what he calls 'the totalitarian menace' which threatens to define freedom in terms of compulsory adherence to particular political or moral principles. The Anglican prayer book, for example, refers to 'perfect freedom' – a state of affairs in which one is only 'truly free' when one has accepted God's grace, the Thirty-Nine Articles and the rest of the paraphernalia of Christian belief. Similarly, 'freedom' for Marxists consists in identifying with the necessary direction of history and with one's inevitable role as participant in the class struggle. The idea of freedom in both instances is truly 'transfigured'. One may become freer by being compelled to recognise the 'truth' of some particular set of religious, moral or political precepts.

Proponents of the negative conception of freedom see this kind of linguistic manoeuvre as a form of politically dangerous 'Newspeak'. George Orwell, it will be remembered, defined the purpose of 'Newspeak' as 'not only to provide a medium of expression for the world view and mental habits proper to the devotees of Ingsoc [English Socialism] but to make other modes of thought impossible – a heretical thought . . . should be literally unthinkable at least as far as thought is dependent on words.' To define the word 'freedom' not in terms of absence of constraint but as freedom to realise other moral, religious or political ends (compulsive rational freedom) smacks of totalitarianism and linguistic jiggery-pokery, so it can be argued.

Charles Taylor, however, holds that such a polemical response is exaggerated and caricatures the concept of positive freedom. Much heat but little light is generated by obsessional, though understandable, concern to protect the purity of language from assault by those seeking to undermine civil liberties. For what 'crude' versions of negative liberty ignore, suggests Taylor, is the existence of a strong philosophical tradition embodied in theorists like Rousseau and Marx in which freedom resides, at least in part, in the 'collective control of life' and is closely associated with ideas of 'self-realisation' or 'rational self-mastery'. Simply to concentrate upon external obstacles to the satisfaction of desires wholly ignores the fact that we may speak quite meaningfully, says Taylor, of 'internal' or psychological constraints. He writes:[3]

> We can't say that someone is free on a self-realisation
> view if, for instance, he is totally unaware of his
> potential, if fulfilling it has never even arisen as a
> question for him or if he is paralysed by the fear of
> breaking with some norm which he has internalised but
> which does not authentically reflect him.

Positive freedom, then, implies that 'one is free only to the extent that one has effectively determined oneself and the shape of one's life' and this means not only freedom from external constraints but an ability rationally to order one's desires so that they do not run 'against the grain of one's basic purposes'.[4]

What I have labelled the 'stark' form of negative liberty and what Taylor prefers to call the 'crude' version of that doctrine implies that a man may properly be held to be free irrespective of his 'internal' state of mind. Proponents of the negative idea of freedom however have been worried by the association of 'freedom' with 'rational self-mastery' or 'self-realisation' since they see the possibility that political or moral authorities may try to 'second guess' the purposes and wants of individuals in a way which is paternalistic and inimical to free individual choice. Suppose, for example, one meets a person who is clearly highly intelligent, musically gifted and who has marked athletic skills who nevertheless rarely exercises those gifts preferring to read mystery stories and imbibe gin and tonics on a regular basis. On the positive view of freedom one is tempted to say that such a person is unfree to the extent that he is not realising his full potential or 'basic purposes'. And even though one may not wish to 'coerce' him into freedom one might say that had he chosen a more 'rational' life his freedom would have been enhanced. And, of course in saying this one would be patronising the individual concerned – 'second guessing' him as to his own basic wants. This kind of superior role, negative theorists would argue, is a dangerous one from a political standpoint and its widespread acceptance would be likely to lead to political paternalism at best or forms of totalitarian control at worst.

Taylor, however, acknowledges that while it may be true that those who know us intimately may be better able to advise us as to our 'real purposes', 'no official body can possess a doctrine or technique whereby they could know how to put us on the rails'[5] – given the diversity of human objectives. Nevertheless it still makes sense to argue says Taylor that freedom is linked to our motives and internal states of minds. We may separate, that is, the political question of whether particular basic purposes ought to be politically enforced in the interests of greater freedom for the individual from the question of the meaning of freedom. An example might help to illustrate the point.

Suppose that I am personally distressed at the activities of my mystery-reading, gin-imbibing friend. Knowing him well, I judge perhaps correctly that he would be happier and more fulfilled if he were to devote more of his time to learning to play the piano, taking a philosophy course, improving his tennis and joining the local Labour Party. I might advise him to do so in the interests of what I conceive of as his 'freedom' without in any way coercing him to be free. This positive conception of freedom then in no way entails, Taylor suggests, that one is justified in coercing people into freedom for our judgment may be in principle at fault. We may, that is, whatever our knowledge of our friend make a mistake about his basic purposes. Nevertheless it is still true, argues Taylor, that the meaning of freedom is necessarily linked to what he calls 'discrimination amongst motivations'. What he means by this is that when we are quite self-deceived or utterly fail to discriminate the ends we seek or have lost self-control we can easily be doing what we want without our being free; indeed we can be further entrenching our 'unfreedom'.

Now this 'positive' way of using the term 'freedom' to include the notion of self-realisation seems to me to be potentially politically dangerous in the sense that it permits the possibility in theory at least if not necessarily in practice of our arguing that external control over individual desire can actually be justified in the name of enhancing liberty. Conceptually speaking 'positive freedom' permits us to impose constraints whilst not viewing those constraints as an interference with individual liberty. Given that there is a standing temptation on the part of politicians and moralists to re-describe interference with liberty as something else – even its contrary – it does seem important to protect within the language a stark negative version of freedom which speaks honestly and unambiguously about constraints – whether justified or unjustified. The difficulty and danger in using positive conceptions of freedom is that *you* may describe justified interference with doing what one wants as increasing my freedom whilst *I* may feel that such actions are unjustified diminutions of my freedom. In your case 'freedom' is being defined in terms of other morally desirable ends, i.e. my 'rationality' or self-discipline, whilst I insist that freedom consists in the lack of interference with what I wish to do. Surely it is preferable to preserve the idea that absence of constraint (i.e. freedom) is a morally desirable end-in-itself, other things being equal, than to insist that freedom be conceptually linked to other possibly desirable principles.

All very well, a critic might suggest, but surely Taylor is right in insisting that one cannot ignore 'internal' constraints

– constraints of the mind as well as constraints of the law and other human agencies? Isn't it an over-simplification to restrict the idea of freedom merely to external constraints upon action and choice? I want to argue the contrary by analysing the senses in which an individual may be 'constrained'.

First, a person may be constrained in the most obvious way by the intentional interference of other human agents. He may, that is, be prohibited by law from acting as he chooses or he may be otherwise threatened with punishment or social sanctions. Such costs are clearly a burden upon him – an interference whether justified or not with his liberty. Second, a person may be constrained through the unintentional consequences which often flow from human action. We live in complex social structures in which the intentions of legislators and others are not always and everywhere fully realised. Indeed much of what we intend to do in one social realm often affects what happens in another. Let us assume for the sake of argument that no legislative body actively intends to place obstacles in the way of the fourth daughter of a manual labourer from Oldham attending Oxford University. Nevertheless it is a statistically demonstrable social fact that in comparison with the only son of a high court judge her chances are minimal. There is a real sense in which this woman's freedom to choose is obstructed by external obstacles even if these are not directly intended by human agents.

Third, we may talk of our being constrained by our own desires in the following possible senses:

(a) we may be subject to 'irrational fears' or compulsions which effectively inhibit us from living out fuller lives;

(b) we may be 'constrained' by what Taylor calls the 'internalisation of norms'. We may, that is, be so committed to particular moral or other evaluational judgments that we effectively prohibit ourselves from engaging in certain activities.

Fourth, we may be constrained in our view of the world by a 'limited conceptual framework'. We may be less than well educated and come to develop false or highly circumscribed opinions about the nature of the social and physical world.

Now within the positive conception of freedom all of these states of affairs – all these multiplicity of constraints – can be said to make us 'less free' but in my view it is highly misleading to argue that the third and fourth categories of 'constraint' here are restrictions upon freedom.

Let me concede at the outset that our use of abstract terms like 'freedom' is not wholly clear and unambiguous. Our language is notable for the possibility of metaphorical extension. Abstract concepts have overlapping boundaries and are sometimes ambiguous and relatively indeterminate. We stretch the meanings of words. One cannot however stretch language indefinitely. Were we to do so we should be unable to think clearly or articulate our common or diverse human purposes. We cannot use language as we like even if we can creatively explore the transfer of one set of ideas into a new context. We cannot for example use the word 'democracy' to refer to the political organisation of the Third Reich and have some difficulty, to say the least, in applying that concept to the so-called German Democratic Republic.

This general point is true of the word 'freedom'. We have in our language clear and unambiguous uses of that word. We can refer to this use as the 'paradigm case' or 'full-blown case' of the application of the concept. Freedom is used unambiguously in its stark negative sense as being the absence of constraint put upon our desires and wants by other human agents. By extension we can also count as obstacles to our freedom those 'social-structural constraints' which are not perhaps directly caused by human intention but which lie outside our control.

The next step in the extension of the notion of constraints upon the realisation of our desires takes us into muddier waters. We might agree with Taylor that an obsessional desire or fixation (say obsessive handwashing or agoraphobia) acts as a constraint upon our freedom since there is a sense in which we can (metaphorically) conceive such a condition as being external to us – something we cannot alter and which appears independent of our will. But here we must surely draw the line or at least indicate the possibility of a boundary which ought not readily to be overstepped. For there is a clear sense in which 'internalisation of norms', for example, is within our conscious control. Unless we are social or psychological determinists (in which case the whole application of the idea of free action is undermined), we have to acknowledge that our evaluations and conceptual frameworks and indeed our capacity for educating our minds and our emotions are potentially or actually within our control. At least it requires special argument to show that our way of viewing the world has been inflicted upon us in the same way that punishment is inflicted upon us by external agencies. There are of course deterministically inclined social theories – like that of classical Marxism which proffer analyses of states of mind viewed as false consciousness in just those kinds of terms – but generally the idea of freedom seems to involve the absence of 'externally imposed' constraints. And we cannot extend the word 'external' indefinitely to all or many of our 'psychic states' without falling into determinism. If I impose constraints upon myself (e.g. I might deliberately place 'obstacles' in my way to enable me to cut down my smoking) I am neither more nor less free in virtue of this action. I have simply decided (freely) to act. The obstacles I place in my way (say, not taking my cigarettes into my classes) don't render me less free nor does the fact of my cutting my consumption of cigarettes to ten a day make me a freer person.

It is with this mistaken metaphorical extension of the notion of freedom to 'internal' states of mind that the proponents of negative liberty are concerned. Such extensions involve not only quasi-determinist interpretations of freedom

– quite the antithesis of the idea of self-realisation incident-ally – but also invite the authoritarian and paternalist to seek to enforce or persuade us to change our mental states in the interests of greater freedom. It may well be that we ought to aim at a more rational life; it may well be that our desires ought to be more coherent, discriminating and purposive. But this has nothing to do with enhancing our freedom in an objective sense. Of course we may feel more free – to stop smoking might be conceived of as a release from a burden – but once again this is a somewhat fanciful metaphor. No one, after all, has intentionally or unintentionally forced us to take up the habit. Self-discipline is not to be equated with freedom or we are indeed upon a slippery path to paradox.

An equally fundamental and perhaps more disturbing as-pect of positive freedom is the insistence that the ideal of freedom 'discriminates between motivations' in the sense that some obstacles to doing what one wants are so trivial that they do not count as interferences with liberty at all.

Charles Taylor argues that commands to obey traffic sig-nals and warnings whilst constituting perhaps a 'philosophi-cal' example of interference with our liberty are not regarded as such in 'serious political debate'. 'We are reluctant', he says, 'to speak here of a loss of liberty at all' in contrast to our response to laws which seek to forbid particular forms of religious worship, for example. He concludes that freedom has a dimension which connotes not only the existence of obstacles but selects amongst those obstacles 'those which are important to man'. To support his contention that one needs to discriminate 'qualitatively' amongst freedoms Taylor con-siders 'a diabolical defence of Albania as a free country'. The argument goes as follows: Albania has abolished religious freedom but almost certainly has fewer traffic regulations than Britain. If one added up, as it were, the sheer number of restrictions upon liberty without considering the significance of the nature of the restrictions one could argue that Albania was as free, if not freer, than Britain. This Taylor suggests is manifestly absurd.

Two comments need to be made here. First, of course, it is true that we do indeed judge some restrictions upon liberties as more important than others. But this does not mean, philosophically, politically or in any other sense that the use of the word freedom is somehow properly restricted only to freedom of religious worship and other freedoms which are 'important to Man'. On the contrary anyone who has driven in a big city knows how traffic regulations can prove extraordinarily frustrating interferences with liberty – as can all bureaucratic regulation which sometimes pays no heed to the particular context of acts but relies upon general rules. In any case, whether an interference with liberty is justified or not, whether it is conceived of as trivial or not it is still an interference with liberty. Of course I may not feel that traffic regulations interfere with my liberty. I may not mind their being put in place. But my state of mind about them surely doesn't alter their status.

The 'diabolical defence of Albania' does indeed seem to me to be diabolical – if the devil uses tautologies to defend his kingdom. What we generally mean – at least what philosophers generally sensitive to civil liberties mean by calling a nation 'a free society' – is just that they respect 'significant' freedoms – freedom of speech, association and assembly. It makes perfect sense however to say 'Albania has less restrictions in general on its citizens than Britain but it is nevertheless not a "free society"' – without implying that the very concept of freedom is restricted to what is significant in the eyes of all good liberals or liberally minded socialists.

What has all this high-flown argumentation to do with practical politics, it might be asked? It has everything to do with politics – both theoretical and practical. What the negative conception of freedom insists upon is the possibility that one can evaluate freedom from external constraint as an end-in-itself irrespective of and distinguishable from other

social, political and moral values. To argue with the proponents of the positive conception that freedom is conceptually restricted by judgments of 'social or moral significance'
or by judgments upon the rationality of ends freely chosen by
the human agent is thereby to devalue the idea of freedom –
to render it in some sense both conceptually and morally
subservient to other ideals. Charles Taylor has indicated
through his clear and well-balanced discussion that we may
trust *him* to be sensitive to the claims of liberty perhaps. But
political principles cannot be applied *ad hominem*. The stark
version of negative freedom serves both intellectual and
political purposes. It enhances clarity of discussion and
simultaneously allows us to argue for the possibility of valu-
ing freedom as absence of constraint as an end-in-itself.

I have argued that there is a tendency on the part of the
political 'left', though by no means exclusively the left, to
fudge the issue of principle over the interpretation of freedom by seeking to collapse the stark negative version into a
more comprehensive formulation of moral principle. This is
a mistake. Socialism is, amongst other things, concerned
with the removal of external obstacles impeding individual
action. There can be no final resolution, social, political
or moral, where clashes occur between competing moral
principles.

But what of the oft-repeated claim that freedom as an
end-in-itself is only protected by the doctrines of the political
right? Here there is an assumption that the so-called 'market
economy' is patently a 'free' form of economic organisation.
A second assumption is that 'freedom in the market place'
also somehow mysteriously protects or is associated with the
civil liberties generally enjoyed by Western Europeans and
North Americans. That there is no demonstrable basis for
such claims is not difficult to show. Indeed as Dr Gerry
Cohen has pointed out, the political right is prone to employ
concepts of freedom which are every whit as value-laden and
distorted as the positive conception of freedom generally

23

recommended by the left. Here again the word 'freedom' is associated with certain value judgments as to what freedoms are significantly worth preserving. At different points in the political spectrum certain kinds of freedom are held to be worth preserving and attempts are then made to show that those particular freedoms constitute the very meaning of the word. Freedom is either the freedom to operate in the market place or it resides in the freedom to live a rationally ordered life.

But, it may be argued, why is this procedure unacceptable? Surely political debate is about differing conceptions of freedom? Why should we seek a more morally neutral conception? Why should we wish to defend freedom – viewed as absence of constraint – as prima facie morally desirable? This raises some fundamental moral questions about the status of high-level moral principles. How indeed are we to justify our deepest convictions and commitments to the significance of such ideas? I have no ready-made answer. Neither 'intuition' nor the numbers of individuals subscribing to this or that principle can ultimately justify our moral claims. It is enough, perhaps, to say, 'I care about constraints upon my free choice and assume that others do likewise.' The negative concept of liberty defines and protects that sense of caring.

(iii) Economic freedom and political liberty

Two decades ago Milton Friedman published a book *Capitalism and Freedom*[6] in which he maintained that economic freedom was a necessary condition of political liberty. He argued that only within the framework of 'competitive capitalism' was it possible to sustain the kind of civil liberties currently enjoyed in the West. Friedman singles out 'democratic socialism' as embodying the 'delusion' that any form of socialism is compatible with individual liberty. He writes,[7] 'a society which is socialist cannot also be democratic in the sense of guaranteeing individual freedom.' For Friedman 'democratic socialism' is literally a contradiction in terms.

This thesis might be thought somewhat extravagant since democratic socialist governments have not in fact appeared to diminish civil liberty. Quite the contrary, it might be argued. Friedman will have none of this. He argues that forms of socialist economic organisation necessarily restrict liberty in the sense that the very structure of socialism generates economic constraints which, as a matter of demonstrable fact, spill over, so to speak, into the political realm.

What variety of 'freedom' is Friedman referring to here? On the abstract level he has endorsed, quite properly, the negative conception of liberty.[8] 'Political freedom', he writes 'means the absence of coercion of a man by his fellow men,' and again, 'freedom . . . has nothing to say about what an individual does with his freedom; it is not an all-embracing ethic.' That is well said. What is at fault in his analysis, however, is that he believes that both political freedom and economic freedom may be construed in the same way. Both, he argues, may be seen as desirable ends since they involve the repudiation of constraints upon human wants and choices. Both are desirable since they are, to him, particular exemplifications of the general moral rule that constraints upon action are prima facie to be condemned. What Friedman and other apologists for competitive capitalism fail to realise, however, is that the use of the adjective 'economic' introduces the idea of constraint as a 'submerged' level of analysis. The argument here is rather complicated and I shall return to it shortly.

Friedman cites as cases of economic 'unfreedom', that is unjustified constraints upon the 'free operation of market forces', the following: the imposition of exchange controls; the compulsory imposition of state pension schemes – what he calls 'retirement contracts' – and price fixing by manufacturers or retailers. These constraints, he asserts, manifestly interfere with consumer choice but also restrict his political liberties, in the sense, say, that severe exchange controls limit one's capacity to travel freely to the countries of one's choice. His argument is that economic and political freedoms are not wholly distinct. Decisions made in one area may, intentionally or otherwise, affect freedom of choice in another. More significantly, Friedman argues, 'history suggests . . . that capitalism is a necessary condition for political freedom'[9] since the tendency towards 'tyranny, servitude and misery' has only been interrupted in the history of man in Athenian and early Roman times and in certain nineteenth and twentieth century societies. These societies, he claims, were and are characterised by free-market economies. He acknowledges however that this historical conjunction, if it be so, is by no means decisive as an argument. What is also significant is that the market place offers a resource, a separate area of activity, through which one can avoid the petty tyrannies of state manipulation. The operation and existence of the market place disperses the concentration of power in the political arm and makes it possible for individuals to resist censorship by 'making a living' independent of political control. There is clearly some modifiable truth in this but Friedman extends this trivial and one-sided argument through a gross simplification of the political process. He asserts that, 'fundamentally there are only two ways of coordinating the economic activities of millions. One is the central direction, including the use of coercion – the technique of the army and of the modern totalitarian state. The other is voluntary cooperation of individuals – the technique of the market place.' He writes that, '*provided the transaction* [within the market-place] *is bilaterally voluntary and informed* [his italics] exchange can bring about coordination without coercion'.[10] This is what he labels 'competitive capitalism'.

There are two points to be made here. First the opposition between a centralised, coerced and totalitarian economy and one in which there is 'voluntary cooperation in the market place' is far from exhaustive of the possible range of economic organisation, as Friedman is well aware. Friedman associates all forms of socialism with the former category. He sees democratic socialism, for example, as involving the adoption of 'the essential features of Russian [Soviet?] economic arrangements', and argues from this that a necessary feature of all forms of socialist economic organisation is the inhibition of civil liberties. This is surely to allow one's 'ideal typifications' of society to dictate one's conception of empirical reality. It is to engage in a process of conceptual manipulation in order to establish what is, after all, a testable empirical thesis. Is it in fact true that all societies which operate with socialist conceptions of government control of the economy thereby abandon their citizens to tyranny? To pose the question is to answer it.

Second, Friedman's conception of 'competitive capitalism' is also 'ideal' – both in the Weberian sense of being a 'one-sided accentuation of empirical reality' and in the moral sense of that word. Can it seriously be maintained that modern 'competitive capitalist' societies are characterised by 'bilaterally and voluntary informed transactions' on the part of its members? Of course not. Friedman is obviously entitled to argue that if, contrary to the fact, this were the case then it is likely that civil liberties would be protected. But to argue for the logical possibility of capitalism sustaining civil liberties is not to show their necessary actual association. His error in logic is compounded when he also stipulates by definition that socialist societies are necessarily committed to the inhibition of political liberty. What set out as an unconvincing historical thesis becomes transformed into an equally unconvincing series of definitional manipulations. To imagine that 'competitive capitalism' is the only form of social and economic organisation which can sustain political freedom surely demonstrates wishful thinking rather than a sustained attempt to grapple with conceptual and empirical realities.

A more fundamental assumption made by Friedman and others of his persuasion is that the case for economic freedom follows as a direct inference from the negative conception of freedom as absence of constraint. This is a piece of erroneous reasoning. It is wholly justifiable both to endorse the notion of negative liberty and yet to deny that economic freedom is a prima facie good.

Let me make it clear that I am not arguing in this context the obvious truth that economic freedom may be justifiably sacrificed to other socially desirable ends like equality. Of course that is always a possibility. Rather, the argument is that 'economic freedom' is not freedom at all in an unambiguous sense of the word. Of course constraints upon economic activities interfere with what some people want to do. The term 'economic freedom', however, incorporates a suppressed or cryptic premiss that certain kinds of constraints upon people are *ipso facto* desirable. That is, to claim 'economic freedom' is necessarily to argue for the justifiable placing of burdens on others. The assumption of the 'free-market' economist is that one has the right to dispose of private property and the freedom to sell one's labour power. But clearly the idea of 'property' in itself – though it is certainly not equivalent to theft – places constraints upon others. I may not use your property freely in virtue of it being 'yours'. Second, although I am in one sense 'free to sell my labour power' there is another sense in which I am forced to do so in a situation of 'economic freedom'.

Dr Gerry Cohen[11] has nicely illuminated and resolved this apparent paradox as follows. Just as Australians are free to vote but not free not to vote, since voting is mandatory in Australia, so under competitive capitalism most workers cannot not work. Clearly although capitalism, in perhaps an ideal form, might put no constraints upon the sale of labour, it forces people to seek employment to live. Cohen argues that there is a sense in which apologists for capitalism and Marxists are both right when they claim respectively that the labourer is free to sell his labour and is forced to do so. The worker under capitalism is not a chattel slave – in this sense he is free from that burden – but he has no alternative but to sell his labour – and in this sense he is constrained.

The point here is that defences of 'economic freedom' imply that this form of social and economic organisation manifestly *lessens* burdens upon the generality of people. Both capital and labour are alleged to be freer than under a socialist economic system. Manifestly this is not necessarily so. Under a system of political liberty however all are (ideally) free to express their opinion or to associate together to pursue their common interests. If I am free to say what I like then I am free in this respect without qualification. I am not forced to give an opinion, write to the newspapers, join a political party or otherwise engage in civic activities. I may choose to do so or not to do so. Of course my freedom of expression may be limited by slander or libel laws but this is seen as an abridgement of my freedom. Under a system of 'economic freedom', however, my freedom is not without qualification. In a free-market economy I am forced to act in particular ways perhaps against my will.

I am not considering here whether these constraints upon my freedom are a good or bad thing. I am making the point (with Cohen) that advocates of economic freedom 'see the freedom which is intrinsic to capitalism but they do not notice the unfreedom which necessarily accompanies it'.

It has been established, then, both that, contrary to Milton Friedman, there is no demonstrable connection between economic and civil liberty and that the idea of 'economic freedom' is a misnomer since advocates of that particular doctrine suppress, or at least fail to notice, the hidden 'unfreedoms' which are associates with it. Through these arguments I have sought to contest and repudiate the claims that the political right has some exclusive or superior notion of what constitutes freedom; that there is a necessary connection between economic freedom and political and civil liberty and that the left needs to develop a more 'positive' or collectivist idea of freedom as a counterweight to the negative conception. I have had occasion to hear academics and politicians, not necessarily on the right, argue the silly thesis that one's point on the political continuum between right and left can be fairly well predicted from one's attitude towards the protection of individual liberty. The more the concern for liberty, so the argument runs, the more likelihood that one will be measurably to the right of centre. To accept this view at any level is to play into the hands of those who believe that the protection of individual liberty is the especial province of conservative politics. It is not; it is one of the firmest planks in a democratic socialist political philosophy.

(iv) Freedom of expression and association: the special case of the propagation of 'racial hatred'

In his classic essay 'On Liberty' John Stuart Mill[12] argued for 'absolute freedom of opinion and sentiment on all subjects, practical or speculative, scientific, moral or theological'.[13] No society, he wrote, could be completely free in which these liberties did not exist 'absolute and unqualified'. These sentiments were directed towards establishing the absolute sanctity of what Mill called 'the inward domain of consciousness'. He argued, however, that the expression and publication of opinions, though not exclusively a private matter, 'is almost of as much importance as liberty of thought' since it is 'practically inseparable from it'. The introduction of the qualifications 'almost' and 'practically' indicate that Mill felt that there were occasions on which liberty of publication, expression and association could be overriden where they led to demonstrable and unequivocal 'harm to others'.

This position has been expressed formally in the statement of principle that individuals shall enjoy the prima facie right to liberty of expression and association but that this right is rebuttable under certain well-defined conditions.

It may appear that this formulation weakens Mill's claim since operation of the qualifying clause might permit authorities drastically to limit individual freedoms whilst simultaneously paying lip-service to the principle itself. Furthermore the omission of any reference to 'absolute and unqualified freedoms', it may be suggested, weakens the very principle itself rendering it ineffective as a substantive declaration of the right to liberty.

There is something in these objections since clearly what is required is a clear and precisely formulated interpretation of the conditions under which freedom of expression and association may be suspended. It should not be overlooked, however, that many governments and political organisations would not, either explicitly or implicitly, give assent to a prima facie right to freedom of expression. They would argue that freedom of speech is not an end-in-itself but that it ought to be linked to the specific content of the belief uttered.

Mill's denial of these authoritarian sentiments and his insistence upon the 'unqualified' right to freedom of expression may be construed as an insistence that the onus is upon those seeking to infringe upon liberty to justify such interference in plain terms. In general what justifies interference is the clear demonstration of unequivocal 'harm to others' which might flow from the exercise of liberty.

The interpretation of the phrase 'harm to others' is obviously crucial here. Mill himself attempted to distinguish between expression of opinion and incitement to harm not by a process of abstract argument or elaborate distinction making but by citing examples which he obviously felt spoke for themselves. He wrote:[14]

No one pretends that actions should be as free as opinions. On the contrary even opinions lose their immunity when the circumstances in which they are expressed are such as to constitute . . . a positive instigation to some mischievous act. An opinion that corn dealers are starvers of the poor or that private property is robbery, ought to be unmolested when simply circulated through the press, but may justly incur punishment

> when delivered orally to an excited mob assembled
> before the house of a corn dealer or when handed about
> among the same mob in the form of a placard.

Such examples have led to the formulation of a distinction between the propagation of heresy and incitement to break the law. It is, however, a moot point whether this distinction can justifiably be employed to restrict the freedoms of un-democratic political groups who publish doctrines advocating the violent overthrow of existing states.

Of course there are cases – exemplified in the laws relating to slander and libel and incitement to injure others – which are reasonably clear-cut. I shall not seek to comment upon these but rather to examine the particular case of whether it is justifiable to suspend certain of the civil liberties of racialist groups like the National Front or the Ku Klux Klan where what is to count as causing 'harm to others' is not so immediately clear.

The first important point to be made is that the liberal and democratic socialist tradition has endorsed the view that under no circumstances is it a sufficient justification to suspend civil liberties merely in response to what one might label 'felt harm'. I may feel injured, disgusted or upset by the expression of racial prejudice, by erotic literature and pictures, by the religious or political opinions of my neighbour or by insulting remarks passed uopn my character or appearance. These are wholly subjective responses and both the law and the liberal tradition has generally rightly held that suppression of fundamental freedoms ought to be based solely upon evidence of objective harm.

Recent race relations legislation in Britain, however, has muddied this previously relatively clear-cut distinction. Section 70 of the 1976 Race Relations Act amends Section 5 of the 1936 Public Order Act so that:

5A   1   A person commits an offence if:

(a) he publishes or distributes written matter which is threatening, abusive or insulting; or

(b) he uses in any public place or at any public meeting words which are threatening, abusive or insulting in a case where, having regard to all the circumstances, hatred is likely to be stirred up against any racial group in Great Britain by the matter or words in question.

Whilst it may be possible perhaps to venture objective criteria for the determination of 'threatening written matter' – as in the sending of a letter which threatens violence against particular individuals or groups – the notions of 'abuse' and 'insult' have irredeemably subjective connotations. Their use, even when restricted within the scope of an act which legislates in the area of 'race relations', is profoundly disquieting.

In fact, however, prosecutions under the Race Relations Act have generally sought to show that publications or speeches of racialist groups were likely to incite 'racial hatred'. As the Labour Party NEC pamphlet of September 1978 – *A Response to the National Front*[15] – points out, however, prosecutions have generally failed to be sustained because of the difficulty in establishing that 'hatred' is likely to be stirred up as a direct consequence of publication of racial abuse. The National Executive of the Labour Party recommended that 'this very strong word' be replaced by the less strong 'racial hostility or prejudice'.

Outside the area of race relations the stirring up of 'hostility and prejudice' is hardly a sufficient criterion for the suspension of civil liberties. Were it so, many politicians, independent of party, would either be languishing in gaol or on indefinite probation and civil liberties would indeed be in a parlous state! In its somewhat confused pamphlet the NEC argues against using public order legislation to suppress National Front assemblies or marches but finally justifies its position on just those criteria of public order and the encouragement of social solidarity it earlier repudiates. The committee writes that whilst being 'fully aware of the dangers involved in introducing legislation of this kind . . . the alternative is to leave the initiative entirely in the hands of those who would seek to promote division in our community and disorder on the streets of our cities and this we cannot accept'.

Who these people are is left vague. We are to assume perhaps that the reference is both to the National Front and to left-wing groups who seek deliberately to disrupt NF assemblies and marches. Appeals to the avoidance of social disorder and division are notoriously illiberal and it is astonishing to see such criteria cited by a democratic socialist assembly. Are there, however, better arguments for the suspension of certain liberties which racialist organisations currently enjoy?

Let me restate the issue. The problem is not one of legislating to prevent racial discrimination but rather one of the justification for legislation so as to prevent the expression of racial prejudice, abuse and insult. The indicators of racial discrimination are reasonably clear and the harm which issues is usually manifest. The local firm in a 'mixed' area which consistently refuses employment to blacks, whether or not there is a declared intent to do so, or the white landlord who uses 'racial' criteria in letting his property, may be easily exposed – although whether prosecution is successful is another matter.

The infliction of 'mental harm' upon racial minorities is a different matter. Here I must repeat that 'felt harm' may under no circumstances serve as the ground for the suspension of civil liberties. I say this very reluctantly since one is only too well aware of the charge that 'white liberals' can afford to indulge the niceties of defending civil liberties when they are largely or wholly immune from systematic racial abuse and harassment. I cannot, of course, share directly the resentments and anger generated periodically or consistently

34

in the minds of those who are the targets of racial slurs. I do know, however, that abuse of this kind is deeply wounding and generates fear, anxiety, hostility and outright violence on the part of those subjected to it. I sympathise with this response which I find to be both explicable and frequently justifiable. Nevertheless, the concept of 'felt harm' which falls short of demonstrable physical abuse or intimidation is too indiscriminate and subjective a concept to use as a criterion for the suspension of civil liberties.

The National Front and the KKK, it may be argued, do not simply engage in organised abuse; they engage in harassment and intimidation. These are manifestly objective harms. The difficulty is however to provide criteria which enables one to distinguish between political propaganda (however nauseous) and acts of harassment or intimidation. Perhaps the distinction cannot be made at the purely abstract level even though one may point to clear-cut examples. If, for example, I make abusive telephone calls to your home at frequent intervals you have legal redress; if I insult you once in the street you probably have not.

The notion of 'provocation', frequently appealed to by those wishing to ban National Front or KKK marches will not fit the bill either. Clearly what provokes one person will not provoke another. The concept is irremediably subjective. A better case might be made for the distinction between 'persuasion' and 'intimidation'. Of course, it may be argued, there are people who are less than robust physically or mentally who may construe the mildest form of persuasion – confident assertion in ringing tones, for example – as intimidation. Nevertheless, if one is prevented from walking the streets from a justifiable fear of probable attack or abuse or if one is prevented from essaying objections to a political viewpoint on the same basis one is clearly intimidated.

The trouble is that this kind of argument can be applied equally to trade union members engaged in lawful picketing. Are we to accept legislation limiting the right to peaceful picketing merely on the grounds that even the strongest of men or women might feel intimidated by the passionate conviction and even anger displayed during a bitter industrial dispute?

Of course it is always tempting to seek to short-circuit these considerations by arguing that in the case of racial abuse or prejudice and only in that case one may justifiably base suspension of civil liberties upon the content of beliefs. It may be suggested that racialist propaganda is self-evidently irrational; that the doctrines propagated by racialists are not amenable to logical and empirical refutation in the sense that no evidence would ever convince a racialist to alter his views. It can be argued that racialists, unlike the trade unionists, are not even in principle engaged in political persuasion. Historical evidence strongly, if not demonstrably, suggests that what is intended is the coercion of racial minorities and their subsequent 'elimination'. Of course, this is in general true. The point is, however, that one cannot just assume it to be true in advance of particular forms of harm being made manifest. Coercion is employed in democratic societies against those who infringe others' freedom or rights only after the event. The notion of the 'preventive' suspension of civil liberties has always been alien to democratic sentiment for once established it is impossible to guarantee that it will not be used against organisations and individuals whose declared policy is the overthrow of the state or even against those whose political programmes may be assumed by the authorities to issue potentially in social harm.

There is a passage in the essay 'On Liberty' which is of singular relevance to this issue. Mill writes of a suggestion that a 'civilisade' be conducted against the Mormon practice of polygamy but one can readily make the necessary changes:[16]

> Let them send missionaries if they please to preach
> against it; and let them, by any fair means (of which

silencing the teachers is not one) oppose the progress of similar doctrines amongst their own people. If civilisation has got the better of barbarism when barbarism had the world to itself it is too much to profess to be afraid lest barbarism after having been fairly got under should revive and conquer civilisation. A civilisation that can thus succumb to its vanquished enemy must first have become so degenerate that neither its appointed priests and teachers nor anyone else has the capacity or will take the trouble to stand up for it. If this be so, the sooner such a civilisation receives notice to quit the better. It can only go on from bad to worse until destroyed and regenerated by energetic barbarians.

One could happily endorse Mill's words but for one salient fact. Mill wrote before the rise of Nazi Germany; before the Holocaust. That single abysmal episode in recent human history must give pause to even the most fervent civil libertarian. It gives pause to me. It is the gross and persistent image of the Final Solution which transforms one's certitude of the rightness of arguments for liberty and toleration into a nagging dilemma. I still cannot adduce any sufficiently compelling argument consistent with libertarian ideals which would support the denial of ordinary civil liberties to the racialist. Yet the symbol of his presence in our political life seems to threaten the very basis for that judgment.

(v) Paternalist legislation

In his essay 'On Liberty' John Stuart Mill wrote of 'one very simple principle' which should 'govern absolutely the dealings of society with the individual in the way of compulsion and control':[17]

> That principle is that the sole end for which mankind are warranted, individually or collectively, in interfering with the liberty of action of any of their number is

self-protection. That the only purpose for which power can be rightfully exercised over any member of a civilised community, *against his will*, is to prevent harm to others. His own good, either physical or moral, is not a sufficient warrant.

Mill goes on to argue that this does not imply that there are no good reasons for remonstrating, reasoning, persuading or entreating someone to follow his long-term interests, or his settled projects, but merely that he ought never to be 'compelled to do or forbear' because it would make him happier, more wise or more rational.

Mill's 'one very simple principle', however, has been criticised in itself and has been subjected to a variety of interpretations generally turning upon the meaning to be given to the phrase 'against his will'.

The word 'will', it has been asserted, is essentially ambiguous. Can we assume that the heroin user takes that drug voluntarily – that he wills the effects which flow from indulging the habit? Doesn't a judgment that someone 'wills' to do something presuppose that he is in a state of 'reflective equilibrium' in which he coolly and rationally surveys the possible consequences of his act? Again doesn't the application of the word 'will' presuppose a settled disposition to act? Isn't the idea of 'willing' opposed to the notion of the arbitrary satisfaction of fleeting desires or whims?

Gerald Dworkin,[18] an advocate of 'positive' conceptions of freedom, has argued, for example, that paternalism may be justified, contra-Mill, if restraint is exercised upon the individual in order that he may live a more rationally ordered life. He advances a 'freedom-maximising test' for paternalism. That is, one is entitled to intervene coercively only to preserve a wider range of freedom for the individual. As we have seen, however, even where this principle pays heed to the 'settled purposes' of the individual the process involves the 'second-guessing' of people's wants and needs by the authorities who seek to enact controlling legislation or by the individual who has the power to control others by threats or by sanctions.

The central difficulty with this principle is that it appears to give too wide a scope for paternalist interference. Not only does it justify for example, the legislation which makes the wearing of safety helmets mandatory for motor cyclists but it can also be invoked in order to ban cigarette smoking, hang gliding and even the ingestion of high-cholesterol foods. Richard Arneson[19] notes that a common failing of such principles:

> is that they fail to safeguard adequately the right of
> persons to choose and pursue life-plans that deviate from
> maximal rationality or that hamper future prospects of
> rational choice.

The pursuit of rationality, suggests Arneson, is, perhaps deplorably, not valued highly by many individuals. Indeed, he notes that 'a vivid reminder that rationality may sometimes be alien to some humans is the circumstance that persons sometimes self-consciously choose to nurture an irrational quirk at the centre of their personalities'.

All concepts of the will which presuppose that one may readily distinguish the 'rational will' from 'mere desire' lend themselves to the articulation and enactment of paternalist legislation. I say 'lend themselves', not 'necessitate', since it is clearly possible to make such a distinction while nevertheless refraining from coercing the desires of individuals into a more rationally ordered pattern.

We may assume with Mill that, in the absence of disabling physical or mental illness, the expressed desires of an individual constitute his 'will'. If this is so, however, isn't it true that much socialist legislation is demonstrably paternalist? One young Liberal acquaintance of mine once referred to socialism as the philosophy of a 'nanny-ridden' society. Such a comment may tell us something of the social background of many young Liberals but the accusation is serious enough to warrant repudiation.

Let me examine, following in part the examples cited by Arneson, a number of cases which might be held to involve paternalist interference:

  (a) an unconscious man is rushed to hospital
  (b) a man is pushed out of the path of an oncoming vehicle
  (c) a law is enacted prohibiting the levelling of usurious rates of interest
  (d) a law is enacted prohibiting individuals entering into slavery contracts
  (e) a law is enacted making compulsory the payment of National Health and pension contributions
  (f) a law is passed enforcing 'closed shop' practices in the steel industry

Clearly cases (a) and (b) are consistent with Mill's principle and are non-paternalist. One may presume that it is the settled purpose of individuals to avoid death and injury. Of course should it turn out that the individuals concerned intended suicide then the act might have to be interpreted *post facto* as paternalist but it is, nevertheless, reasonable to assume on grounds of probability that force exerted to save a life would be welcomed rather than resisted by the persons concerned.

In cases (c) and (d) one is surely right to make the assumption, in the light of probability, that contracts which involve giving oneself over to slavery or placing oneself in the hands of extortionate money lenders arise not from free consent but from the inequality of powers between the contracting individuals. Sanctions against such contracts are clearly non-paternalistic.

Arguments for compulsory membership of National Health or pension schemes may be paternalist or non-paternalist and it is important for socialists to argue the latter case. The argument that many individuals are feckless and unable to order their affairs or to provide for their future even if true provides no justification for mandatory insurance schemes. The non-paternalist argument for such schemes rests upon two empirical premisses. First is the demonstrable inequality of power and wealth which effectively prohibits many lower-paid workers from safeguarding the health of their families, and second that without the element of compulsion it would be impossible to organise efficient health schemes. NHS legislation is justified not on the grounds that individuals are unwilling to provide for their health needs but that they are virtually unable to do so. The state here is not in the role of 'a nanny' but directly serves the interest of the wills of individuals. Where such legislation runs counter to some individual wills – generally the wills of members of those social classes who are able to provide for their future without undue stress – the justification for coercion needs to be expressed in terms of the prevention of public harm.

Mandatory legislation to enforce trade union 'closed shops' is also capable of being interpreted as non-paternalist. It is no justification to argue that non-union workers do not understand their true interests – again, whether this is true or false. What is at issue is whether the infringement of the liberty not to join a union is justified in terms of the general benefit which accrues to the least advantaged section of the working class. Given the vast inequalities of power between the unorganised worker and organised capital this infringement of liberty appears wholly justified. One would hope, however, that with the introduction of more egalitarian social policies this freedom would be restored.

In general, what is often seen as paternalist legislation may be properly defended in straightforward utilitarian terms – the promotion of public benefit and the amelioration of public harm. This is not to argue, however, that such legislation is necessarily justified by an appeal to 'utility'.

Paternalist arguments for legislative practice are always subversive of civil liberties in that they represent coercion as being in the interests of extending freedom. No democratic socialist, whatever the temptation, should have truck with such considerations. Socialists ought to seek to minimise the degree of coercion consistent with the promotion of manifest public benefit. Legislation within a democracy derives its authority not from 'the pater' or the maternal surrogate of the upper classes – the nanny. Indeed these symbolic figures often undergo a sea-change when their authority is indulged. They turn into Big Brother.

2 Equality and fraternity

'He wants no servants under him
and no boss over his head.'

BERTOLD BRECHT, Song of the United Front'

'Strive, if thou canst to make good thy station on the upper deck;
those that live under hatches are ordained to be drudges and
slaves. . . . Poverty is a shame amongst men, an imprisonment of
the mind, a vexation of every worthy spirit.'

SIR WALTER RALEGH, 'Instructions to his Son'

(i) Inequality, poverty and hierarchy

These two quotations express two elements central to the
idea of equality – a moral condemnation of both hierarchy
and poverty. For Bertolt Brecht, as for all socialists, what is
demanded is the ultimate abolition of inequalities of power
and status; for Ralegh poverty is an inevitable social evil
which is best avoided. Given that there must be bosses and
servants it is better to stand on the 'upper deck'. Whether or
not Brechtian egalitarianism is a pipe-dream and whether or
not Ralegh's view of the world was and is unnecessarily
pessimistic or cynical is a moot point. Suffice it to say here
that across a wide spectrum of political beliefs the necessity
for some form of social inequality is accepted. I hope to
demonstrate later that this consensus is mistaken.

Inequality and poverty are not the same thing. It is a

mistake to equate them or to assume that the one is a necessary correlate of the other. Even though in all known societies
inequality is actually associated with widespread poverty this
need not be the case. It is possible to imagine a society in
which there were wide disparities of reward but little or no
genuine deprivation. Of course all hierarchies may generate a
sense of relative deprivation – a desire on the part of the less
privileged to match the rewards granted to those better
placed. This fact is consistent, however, with the 'least
advantaged' class enjoying a high standard of material com-
fort.

For many 'moderate' conservatives and liberals such a
hierarchically ordered society which guarantees a pleasant
and civilised life to all, whilst simultaneously rewarding
merit and enterprise, is the best that we can reasonably hope
for. They argue that it is not inequality *per se* that is an evil;
rather it is the deprivation and poverty which results from
certain forms of the unequal distribution of resources and
respect which calls for remedy. This 'middle of the road' view
may be illustrated by a simple, schematic example. Suppose
we have good evidence for supposing that the mode of production in a given society 'C' will make twenty units of some
material good available for distribution whilst a 'less efficient'
social system 'S' can produce only nine of those units. Suppose society 'C' to be tolerant of inequities and society 'S' to
be strictly egalitarian. Which society is morally preferable?
In society 'C' due to the combined operation of market forces
and government intervention the actual distribution of
'goods' across the three major classes may run as follows:
upper class – 10 units; middle class – 6 units; lower class – 4
units. In society 'S' all groups receive 3 units apiece.

Surely it may be argued society 'C' is to be preferred since
its system of rewards encourages enterprise and makes
everybody better off. Inequalities in 'C' are justified, it may
be suggested, only if they lead to a real improvement in the
condition of the least advantaged class. The commitment of

society 'S' to an egalitarian form of distribution is thus made to appear quixotic – even pure folly.

The trouble with this simple example is that, even if we accept its dubious and politically loaded assumptions about the relative economic superiority of system 'C', we cannot accept its narrow conception of human satisfaction. Hierarchical relationships in society are intrinsically demeaning. They diminish the human potentiality for autonomy, self-respect and personal growth. They encourage both authoritarianism and a response of deference based upon class, status or office rather than a response of respect based upon genuine worth or ability. Hierarchical social structures generate orthodoxy of opinion and hinder innovation and, often, policies and practices are developed which serve only to perpetuate social division rather than to meet people's needs.

Even if one accepts the dubious proposition that a hierarchical society promotes greater economic efficiency it is still the case that inequalities have intrinsic demerit. This fact needs to be taken into account in any theoretical discussion of competing political evaluations.

I have argued that, on the theoretical level, there is no necessary link between the existence of inequalities and poverty. This is, however, an abstract argument uninformed by empirical realities. As Professor Ted Honderich points out, in discussing the idea of equality we need to start from the fact of existing inequalities. We need to address, initially, not the formal analysis of concepts but the evidence that we have plainly before us that the unequal distribution of the world's resources is a prime factor in the initiation and persistence of massive poverty.

Honderich[1] cites the following figures for life-expectancy at birth for individuals living in poor countries as against those living in richer parts of the world.

He comments that about half the world's population has average lifetimes twenty-nine years shorter than another

	Gabon	Guinea	Nigeria	India	Colombia
Male	25	26	37	42	44
Female	45	28	37	41	46

	France	West Germany	America	England & Wales
Male	69	67	67	69
Female	76	73	75	75

quarter of the world. When the quality of these 'lifetimes' is taken into account it becomes obvious that misery, degradation, powerlessness, illness and early death are the lot of a considerable portion of mankind. Why this is so is a complex matter but clearly one vital element in the 'poverty equation' is the factor of the grossly uneven distribution of the world's resources. The present complex of independent or inter-dependent economies appears unable or unwilling to harness world production and distribution to alleviate the lot of half the world. Indeed in strongly criticising the widely acclaimed Brandt Report 'North-South: A Programme for Survival', Richard Gott of the *Guardian* newspaper commented that its reliance upon 'the same old developmentalist nostrums' ignored the fact that the existence of the world capitalist economic system 'strengthens those local elites, frustrates indigenous development and hinders the overthrow of barbaric and anti-popular regimes. It promotes and perpetuates the misery and deprivation in which so much of the world's population now lives.'

Gott's thesis, and by implication that of Honderich, is that international inequality is not simply the outcome of the unintended operation of inexorable causal economic laws; rather it is, in a major degree, a consequence of the direct intentions of those dominating the operation of the world economy. Inequalities are deliberately sustained or allowed to flourish, so it is argued, to promote the interests of a variety of ruling groups in spite of the clear evidence that the continuance of national and international hierarchies subverts the lives of millions.

One need not, however, appeal solely to international inequities for even in the most privileged of nations and in spite of so-called 'safety-net' or welfare legislation poverty remains a real and depressing reality for a substantial section of the populace.

The facts of national and international poverty are documentable truisms. But they are truisms which many of us prefer not to think about, let alone act upon. Why is this so?

Honderich gives at least part of the answer by comparing our typical emotional responses to the facts of violence and inequality respectively. When faced with the facts of violence, Honderich argues, we respond in an *active* way. We feel disgusted, vengeful, angry or experience deep repugnance. We are drawn towards active condemnation. Contrast these responses with those experiences when we are told of the existence of inequalities with their consequent or concomitant human distress. In these cases we tend to experience a passive response. We feel sad, weary, bitter, resigned or merely resentful. Indeed, suggests Honderich, the very use of the label 'inequality' acts as an 'anodyne' which numbs our sensibilities to the facts of human pain.

The reason for the difference in response, Honderich suggests, is, first, that inequality appears distant and impersonal. Those 'responsible' for inequality are not easily identifiable – as is for example the perpetrator of a violent crime. Second, inequalities are perhaps more familiar to those of us living relatively secure lives than are the facts of violence. Furthermore inequality seems both entrenched and a concomitant of order. Hierarchy is associated with stability and predictability of expectation so that its impact upon us is attenuated. We may come to feel, with Kant, that 'inequality is a rich source of much that is evil but also of everything that is good'.

Furthermore the very vocabulary of the social sciences –

the metaphors of structure and stratification – tend to make us think of inequality as a 'fact of nature' – as external to us and basically unalterable by man in the social world as 'stratification' is in the world of geology or physical geography.

What all this amounts to, suggests Honderich, is that we often temper our response to the evils of inequality because we make a number of unwarranted assumptions prior to addressing the question. It is as if we provide ourselves with a form of perceptual insulation from the worst evidences of human degradation. We may be seduced into thinking that inequalities are unavoidable, necessary or even desirable in part. Only if we strip from the word 'inequality' these debatable assumptions can we respond appropriately to the range of human misery implicit in the very idea.

Merely to recommend an increased sensitivity to existing inequalities is not sufficient, however, to characterise egalitarianism. What is needed is a cogently formulated set of principles which does justice to the 'full-blown' conception of equality which both repudiates other and 'weaker' and misleading conservative and liberal formulations and which meets the objections of critics. In entering into this complex and abstract inquiry we shall see that differing conceptions of the nature of equality are linked to differing political opinions about its possibility or desirability. I shall argue that there is only one coherent notion of equality which does full justice to the facts of inequality and to the dimensions of any proposed remedy.

(ii) Equality as impartiality of consideration

On one view of the idea of equality radical egalitarianism is seen as absurd. Since people everywhere differ in abilities, potential and needs, the major emphasis, it is argued, should not be placed on the question 'how can we treat people more equally?' but upon 'what are the relevant differences which justify us in treating people unequally?'

S.I. Benn and R.S. Peters,[2] for example, argue that: 'Out of context equality is an empty framework for a social idea; it has content only when particularized.' In other words, claims to equality need to be interpreted as a protest that the wrong criteria are being used to justify existing inequalities. This cautious liberal approach towards equality is closely linked to the Popperian idea of 'social engineering'. Absolute equality of distribution of the 'material means to happiness', it is argued, is wildly utopian and flies in the face of the facts of human motivation. On this view it is better to direct our questioning to inequalities that are of social significance in the real world – unequal treatment in virtue of one's 'race', sex or physical handicap, for example. If it can be shown that such discriminations have no moral basis then we may recommend their abolition as soon as is politically practical. In this way assaults upon unjustified inequalities are carried out piecemeal and with care and deliberation.

There is, however, according to Benn and Peters, a perfectly general sense connoted by the idea of equality. It is, they argue, a form of high level principle of impartiality. They write:[3]

> What we really demand when we say all men are equal
> is that *none shall be held to have a claim to better*
> *treatment than another in advance of good grounds being*
> *produced*.

In other words, if I wish to treat you differently or unequally or to discriminate in your favour or against you I need to produce good arguments. If there are none, or if my grounds are 'inadequate', then there remains a 'prime facie right' to equality of treatment.

An application of this idea of equality might work as follows. Suppose I have a bar of chocolate which I want to share between my children. Generally speaking, unless I specify that the chocolate is a reward for some meritorious act there are no good grounds for my preferring a rule of distribution other than 'equal shares'. Suppose however that I have to make a decision, given my limited resources, upon which of my children ought to be supported at university for four years. Suppose further that one of my children is male and the others female. That fact alone is not a sufficient ground for discrimination. But I may produce arguments directed towards showing that higher education is a 'better investment' for a boy rather than a girl; that girls are by nature less 'intellectual' than boys; that they are unlikely to be primarily responsible for their own upkeep; and so forth. Having so argued I can then maintain that my decision to prefer my son is perfectly compatible with a generalised commitment to a principle of equality. In this case, I can argue I have good grounds for overriding the prima facie principle of impartiality of consideration in a way which was not available to me when I distributed chocolate.

Of course, these arguments could be strongly resisted and be shown to rest on false assumptions (as they undoubtedly are). Nevertheless on the present analysis they are granted status as 'candidate good reasons' for discrimination.

The flexibility of this approach which allows for an almost open class of 'good grounds' to be seriously entertained as overriding the prima facie case for equal treatment lies in the fact that the general principle of equality has little or no substance. As J.D. Lucas comments:[4]

> the Principle of Formal Equality does not provide of itself any criteria of relevance; it does not by itself establish much. It gives a line of argument but not any definite conclusion.

According to Benn and Peters, however, certain kinds of justification are deemed to be logically inconsistent with the so-called 'procedural principle of impartiality of consideration'. For example, it would not do to cite as a reason for discrimination mere membership of a particular class. The rule does not permit me, that is, to argue for favoured treatment on the grounds that I am Keith Dixon, male, white and a university teacher. To claim that specific group membership is associated empirically with other relevant features is, however, a further question. Thus the rule of impartiality would not necessarily rule out in advance arguments adduced to show, for example, that white, male university teachers are genetically superior or more worthy of merit than other classes of person. Everything would hang upon whether one could make this argument stick!

What this version of the idea of equality entails, then, is that we are committed to work towards a society where inevitable inequalities of treatment are rationally justified. What is considered rational is dictated by our moral point of view, by rigorous argumentation and by sound empirical evidence. The principle of equality is thus 'minimally substantive'. By itself it gives us little direct guidance as to which particular inequalities are just or unjust. Rather it places the burden of justification squarely upon the shoulders of those who wish to discriminate.

It may at first sight appear that, viewed in this light, the procedural principle of equality is neutral as between political evaluations or political parties. It seems possible either to deny the relevance of current justifications for inequality or to affirm them – given sufficient reasons. But this appearance of political neutrality is superficial. The idea of 'procedural inequality' begs a number of moral and political questions. The 'minimally substantive' status of the general principle directs our attention towards the justification of inequalities rather than to their abolition. The emphasis is significant. Behind it lies the assumption of cautious liberals that any form of radical egalitarianism is so much cloudy utopianism. Sensible men and women, it is implied, will have no truck with dreams or nightmares of total equality and all that nonsense. What is needed is rational assessment of what particular discriminations are sound or unsound. Concentrate upon that and we can get forrader without becoming bogged down in vague generalities and misconceived hopes. One can almost hear the voices of tough-minded university committee men and administrators impatient with the 'posturing' of student radicals.

Of course a further assumption behind this 'liberal' view of equality is that sensible people will agree upon what constitutes relevant differences which justify discrimination. Such justifications will, in general, make reference to ideas of 'desert' and 'entitlement' and I shall return to discuss these notions later. What is ignored or seriously underestimated is the extent to which all existing inequalities of treatment are deeply suspect from a moral point of view. The suspicion of the egalitarian is insufficiently captured in the principle of impartiality of consideration. What the radical egalitarian insists upon is the case for the abolition of inequalities many of which are deeply entrenched in a social system in which the 'rationality' of certain inequalities is taken-for-granted.

I am aware that, in what I have just written, there is an element of the *ad hominem*. I have suggested that some of the deeply embedded assumptions of this view of equality can be traced to the social and political milieu in which they were articulated. I am far from suggesting, however, that such considerations invalidate this particular analysis of the concept. Rather, I suggest both that radical egalitarianism has not been given a fair crack of the whip and that Benn and Peters's view of the nature of equality is simply mistaken. It is of course a serious and conceivably sustainable piece of political reasoning – but it is not about equality.

(iii) John Rawls's conception of equality: relegation to Third Division status?

Professor John Rawls in his monumental book *A Theory of Justice*[5] seeks not only to analyse the meaning of the notions of freedom and equality but to provide general criteria for ordering them. What he suggests is a rule which, crudely speaking, implies that in a 'nearly just' society principles of individual liberty may always be taken to override principles of equality. In any particular case, that is, if we are forced to choose between freedom of association, for example, and remedying poverty then we should ensure freedom first.

Rawls assumes that Western industrial democracies come a good way to meeting the ideal of a just society. Hence his book is both an analysis of political ideas and, simultaneously, a piece of political reasoning directed towards justifying certain forms of political obligation to his readers in virtue of their citizenship.

Rawls is a 'root and branch' thinker. He elaborates and defends his conclusions in over 600 pages of tightly knit, sometimes technical and often repetitive arguments. Reading Rawls is rather like traversing a complex landscape. First the major features of the terrain become apparent and then one is invited to immerse oneself in the details only to return to survey the scene with greater understanding of the interlocking elements. It is an arduous journey during which one often feels the need of a competent guide.

In trying to précis Rawls's ideas one is inevitably guilty of simplification and omission. Nevertheless there are clear and direct conclusions to be drawn from his work – conclusions about both the relative status of the ideas of freedom and equality and of their political import.

Rawls's key notion is that one may deduce one's political and moral obligation from the notion of rational self-interest. The metaphor Rawls uses to express this deduction is a familiar one in political philosophy. He imagines a group of people who come together to reflect upon what set of political principles should serve as the 'Archimedian point' for judging the structure of the coming society.

The individuals, so imagined, are not yet part of any existing society but they share a number of characteristics in virtue of their common humanity. Rawls proposes that they will be self-interested, equal to one another in their freedom to advance opinions and rational – in the sense that they understand the relationship between the ends they seek and the means appropriate to their realisation. Further, they are free from malice and envy towards others and have a clear, general understanding of the springs of human behaviour and of the various sciences which contribute to this understanding.

What is absolutely crucial to their characterisation, however, is that they are wholly in ignorance of their own individual future in the society to come. Each knows nothing of his own possible or probable economic or social position nor of his own potentialities – mental or physical. The judgment of each is deemed to be objective and 'considered' – undertaken, that is, in a state of 'reflective equilibrium' undisturbed by prejudice, wishful thinking or emotional tumult.

Rawls is not suggesting, of course, that these paragons of 'rationality' exist or have actually existed. Nor is it important that there is an obvious inconsistency in claiming that such people are both very clever and emotionally well-balanced but yet remain in ignorance of that fact about themselves. The idea of placing people in this 'Original Position', as it is often called, is a metaphor for Rawls's concept of human rationality. Let us assume, he is saying, that individuals are rationally self-interested but not necessarily benevolent or altruistic, and see if we can, upon this limited assumption, deduce the possibility of a decently ordered society.

What sort of society, then, would such people recommend and upon what basis?

A rational man, suggests Rawls, would not gamble with his own future prospects. He would opt for a form of society in which, were he to occupy the lowest rank, he would be better off and better protected than in alternative societies. He would choose, that is, the security of modest well-being over the chance of great wealth or poverty. Since individuals share similar characteristics in the 'Original Position' – a fact that

54

has led some critics to question the point of positing an assembly of persons at all – a man choosing for himself chooses for all.

What other social 'goods' might a man seek to foster and to protect? Primarily, answers Rawls, he would seek to protect his liberty. Whatever his social or economic position the rights freely to express his opinions, to assemble where he chooses for peaceful purposes and the right to own personal property are of greatest value. This constitutes the deduction of Rawls's *Principle of Liberty*. It is a familiar one in the history of liberal thought, deriving of course from John Stuart Mill's classic formulation in 'On Liberty'. Rawls writes:[6]

> Each person is to have an equal right to the most extensive total system of equal basic liberties compatible with a similar liberty for all.

This principle overrides all others. For Rawls it is 'freedom first'. Interference with the traditional liberties of the individual is never to be justified by an appeal to countervailing demands to ameliorate poverty or to enforce a more egalitarian distribution of social goods.

Is equality unimportant, then, for Rawls? Not at all. Though not of first importance it has much relevance to the articulation of a just society.

Rawls assumes, it is fair to say, that there will, of necessity, be differences in the distribution of social and economic goods and services. Hence he labels his principle of equality the 'Principle of Difference'. This change of designation is highly significant! Rawls's conception of equality is more nearly consistent with that of Benn and Peters than with so-called 'radical egalitarianism'. There are two points of similarity. First, Rawls echoes Benn and Peters's view that equality is the 'normative baseline'. All inequalities, that is, need to be justified on good grounds. Second, there is throughout Rawls's work no serious entertainment of the view that a 'classless society' is a possibility.

Rawls's analysis of his Principle of Difference falls into two parts. The first is implied in Rawls's contention that rational men do not gamble unnecessarily with their future prospects. They operate, that is, with a 'Maximin' principle – 'choose the best of the worst possible cases.' From this it follows that the 'least advantaged class' in a society ought to be protected and that:[7]

> Social and economic inequalities are to be arranged so that they are . . . (a) to the greatest benefit of the least advantaged.

This means that, for Rawls, a class-divided society is only permissible or justified if it is both a precondition of and has the effect of improving the lot of the poorest members. A stratified society in which the poor are reasonably well provided for is to be preferred, according to Rawls, to a more egalitarian society which permits or entails poverty for its worst-off class.

It is important to note that this first part of Rawls's Principle of Difference (Equality) actually makes the existence of a better-off class obligatory if that is the only way of raising the level of the worst-off. One is reminded of the notorious economic justification of inequality based upon the so-called 'trickle down effect'. The more money, opportunity and status rewards given to the rich, it is argued, the more likely it will be that their economic initiatives will benefit the poor in the long run. To be fair to Rawls, however, this is a vulgar parody of this part of the Principle of Difference.

As Ted Honderich rightly remarks, however:[8]

> It is . . . a logical possibility that the principle be satisfied in a society of no social and economic inequality whatever, in a society of overwhelming inequality or in any society in between.

Inequalities, according to Rawls's Principle of Difference,

can *always* in principle be justified. The contrary is true, however, for the Principle of Liberty!

The second part of the Principle of Difference has, paradoxically, general priority over the first part. This formulation reads:[9]

> Social and economic inequalities are to be arranged so
> that they are . . . (b) attached to offices and positions
> open to all under conditions of fair equality of
> opportunity.

This second principle of equality of opportunity stand *above* the principle that the least advantaged class must benefit from inequality in society. It is not permissible, according to Rawls, to improve the lot of the poor if this involves denying or restricting opportunities to other members of the society. This principle would presumably exclude, at least prima facie, programmes of 'affirmative action' or 'reverse discrimination'. In order to justify these social policies one would, at the very minimum, have to demonstrate that current opportunities were distributed 'unfairly' owing to discrimination against various groups in the past.

For Rawls, then, the Principle of Liberty has absolute priority. Equality of Opportunity stands next in the hierarchy and the remedying of the lot of the worst class last of the three.

But what of Rawls's conception of the idea of equality? He seems to assume that equality is merely about 'fair opportunity' or remedying poverty. But just as inequalities do not necessarily involve poverty, the remedying of poverty is not all that there is to equality!

It bears repeating continually that claims to equality, whilst they may in part be directed towards remedying the unfair distribution of resources, are, more importantly, a recognition of the intrinsic undesirability of hierarchy. Rawls thinks it 'unreasonable', even irrational, of men to prefer a state of relatively less material benefit in the interests of

greater freedom from the constraints and indignities of hierarchy. His analysis in this respect misses the point. For Rawls
there is nothing wrong with inequality as long as it produces
the goods, so to speak, for the lower orders. Radical egalitarians want another and a different thing. They want a
'republic of equals'.

(iv) Radical egalitarianism

Radical egalitarianism is the doctrine that people ought to
have equality of power, authority, control, respect and
material condition. It is the only political credo that takes the
claim to equality seriously. Radical egalitarianism does not
restrict itself to the notion that we must treat equals equally
and unequals unequally; nor does it focus upon the justification of *in*equalities. It demands, prima facie, equality of
satisfaction and respect, where that is responsive to social
action, without consideration of desert or entitlement. It
does not however envisage society as a grey, formless mass of
undifferentiated individuals shorn of distinctiveness and
eccentricity. Neither does it recommend a deadening same-
ness of experience. On the contrary, the virtue of egalitarian
principles is to stress that through the removal of inequalities
individuals may autonomously follow their own different
interests and life plans.

The term 'radical egalitarianism' was first coined, as far as
I am aware, by Professor Kai Nielsen. He appends the
adjective 'radical' in order to distinguish his view from the
supposed egalitarianism of John Rawls and others. I have
retained this expression although, in one sense, the word
'radical' is redundant.

Nielsen defines the two major principles of radical egalitarianism as follows:[10]

(1) Each person is to have an equal right to the most
extensive total system of equal basic liberties and

opportunities (including opportunities for meaningful work, for self-determination and political participation) compatible with a similar treatment of all.

(2) After provisions are made for common social values, for capital overhead to preserve the society's productive capacity and allowances are made for differing unmanipulated needs and preferences, the income and wealth (the common stock of means) is to be so divided that each person will have a right to an equal share. The necessary burdens requisite to enhance well-being are also to be equally shared, subject, of course, to limitation by differing abilities and differing situations [attributable to] natural environment not class ·positions.

What precisely is entailed in these complex principles? Let me begin by elaborating the 'moral surround' so to speak through which these principles have meaningful political application.

Nielsen's view is that equality is desirable in its own right, but, more importantly, that existing inequalities stand in the way of human self-realisation and autonomy. In Nielsen's own words what is of first importance is 'what [equality] brings about in terms of human flourishing'. Equality for him is a 'positive' concept. It entails not merely the release from constraints upon what one desires but, further, the incorporation of a moral ideal. That ideal is the vision of a society in which people are encouraged to pursue intellectual, aesthetic and physical activities for their own sake within a cooperative, humane and unselfish framework.

Egalitarianism can only work, Nielsen suggests, under circumstances radically different from those prevailing in any existing society. Individuals would live 'under conditions of moderate abundance'; they would have a secure life; they would not be greedy 'accumulators or possessive individuals'; the aim of their economy would not be profit maximisation but 'the satisfaction of the human needs of everyone'. Furthermore industrial and political democracy would flourish in a spirit of cooperation rather than competition.

In this, admittedly radically different society the principles of just distribution and equal respect would be applied, according to Nielsen, as follows:

First, 'social status' would be abolished or minimised. Respect, honour and reward would not be attached to particular social roles (doctor, lawyer, politician, artisan and so forth) but to individuals. All basic civil liberties would be guaranteed and would be equally protected without reference to class position.

Second, certain crucial social commitments would have to be met from the 'common stock'. Proper health services, pensions and compensation payments would have to be funded as would programmes in education and the arts for example. The society would also need to fund capital intensive industrial and agricultural programmes so that 'moderate abundance' could be sustained. After these basic societal needs were met, the residue of the 'common stock' would be distributed equally according to people's 'unmanipulated needs and preferences'. What is meant here is that in any egalitarian society individuals will differ in what they want. These individual differences, however, would not be predicated upon or sustained by the machinery of commercial mass persuasion. Rather such needs would be 'genuine' – flowing from the individual's personal preferences which would be linked to his own distinctive life plans. Given that individuals differ in their interests and capacities, each would take from the common stock only what he needed. This would mean that some would take more than others, some less. The criteria for distribution would not, however, be 'ability to pay' but 'ability to benefit'. Under present social arrangements 'ability to benefit' (from education, say) is class-biased. If we assume, however, that certain abilities, talents and energies are at least in part 'genetically' or 'naturally' given or are the product of 'unmanipulated' parental love and guidance then those talents may require to be more extensively fuelled from the common stock. Particular natural aptitudes, talents or energies would also carry with them increasing responsibilities to give more time, thought and effort to the common good.

It is important to note that Nielsen does not believe that this complex system of distribution would of necessity require a highly centralised bureaucracy. Rather the distribution system would work upon the basis of democratic management by all working people. Certainly government agencies would be required but those would not, by and of themselves, set social goals or criteria of distribution. What Nielsen envisages is a cooperative society in which a myriad 'local democracies', whether political, industrial, agricultural or artistic, would work in relative harmony with the 'organs of the State' or, as he suggests, the organs of the community. This does not mean, for Nielsen, however, that social conflict would disappear but that conflict based upon class division would be minimised or rendered unnecessary.

The practical implementation of such an egalitarian society would be an onerous undertaking. Mistakes would be made and injustices perpetrated. Nevertheless, Nielsen clearly takes seriously the possibility of realising such a society given the good will of all.

What are we to make of all this?

For the so-called 'hard left', of course, such quasi-utopian principles could only be realised after a political and possibly military victory over 'the entrenched forces of reaction'. They argue for a 'transitional stage' during which civil liberties would have to be suspended; in which modified forms of working-class dictatorship would be necessary; in which political 'education' or indoctrination processes would have to be set in train. The problem with 'transitional stages', however, is that the process of transition often takes an unconscionable time. What becomes 'entrenched' are new and less remediable forms of social control, exploitation and injustice.

Nielsen, on the contrary, argues that justice as equality needs to be realised 'by moral argumentation in the public sphere'. Such argument, he notes, will be firmly resisted and not given a fair hearing. In the end argument may not prevail. Nevertheless, the alternatives – violent revolution and/ or the imposition of egalitarianism upon working people by intellectual and political elites – runs clear counter to the very spirit of that doctrine.

My own view of radical egalitarianism places the emphasis differently. Nielsen, perhaps, allows himself to be seduced into trying to answer the question 'what would an egalitarian society look like and what are the preconditions of its realisation?' The sketching of a possible *picture* of an egalitarian society, however, whilst being an interesting intellectual pursuit, gives unnecessary hostages to fortune.

For the 'hard-Marxist' left this allegedly utopian undertaking can be portrayed as so much ideology – a bourgeois intellectual indulgence actually functioning to divert interest and concern away from the material and economic basis of society into some free-floating vision of the moral good. For a wide range of so-called 'centrist' opinion, such defences of egalitarianism are seen as wildly utopian, politically impractical, contingently subversive of civil liberties, against 'nature' and evidence of the political naivety of socialists generally.

We do not, however, have to start with some general picture of what an egalitarian society would look like. We *can* 'start from where we are' – taking into account the structure of existing inequalities and the associated social and individual attitudes which sustain them.

The more appropriate metaphor for the egalitarian is that of 'continuous exploration of a terrain' rather than that of representational art. In the process of exploration we need to have a rough idea of the kind of terrain upon which it would be appropriate to build. We need rough and ready guidelines and a compass which will indicate when we are going in the wrong direction. The changing terrain may cause us to modify our plans – perhaps to compromise in order to meet limited objectives. During our exploration we may encounter new geological facts which are resistant to easy alteration. But most important of all we are constantly encountering evidence left by those who have gone before as to what terrain to avoid.

Put into less metaphorical language, we know that in-equalities exist. We know that inequalities are disabling. We know that hierarchy constrains our freedoms. We do not know the precise extent to which human attitudes are the products of social and economic forces alone nor can we foresee the extent to which something called 'the state' will need to intervene to promote and to sustain an egalitarian society. We need to start the process of reform piecemeal – where and when we have sound understanding and limited predictability. This means a concerted programme of oppo-sition to existing inequalities and a programme of 'public argumentation' designed to remove artificially raised barriers to a full understanding of the egalitarian case.

Thus, in my view, the present burden upon the egalitarian is largely negative rather than positive. Arguments need to be adduced against present inequalities, against uninformed or merely 'ideological' criticisms of the very possibility of a classless society. As these impediments are removed so we shall be that much closer to realising what is socially possible within the framework of egalitarian principles. We need, not a blueprint, but a staking out of the ground. Nielsen's prin-ciples of radical egalitarianism are better construed in the latter rather than the former sense.

(v) Objections and impediments to radical egalitarianism

There are, at the minimum, four serious objections to radical egalitarianism. The first of these involves questioning the very basis of the value of equality. Upon what grounds, it may be asked, do we believe that greater equality in the conditions of life is desirable? Surely, the argument runs, we cannot start from scratch by accepting some utopian moral rule. All actual societies have a complex history and social structure in which inequalities are deeply embedded. Some of these may be justified by entitlement, desert or by the exercise of 'natural' abilities and assets. Why should we assume, a priori, that all inequality is prima facie unjustified? Surely all reasonable men would agree that hard work, intelligence and moral virtue ought self-evidently to be differentially rewarded over sloth, stupidity and wickedness.

Second, it may be argued, even if greater equality were desirable in itself, the cost of establishing and enforcing laws guaranteeing equality would involve a degree of state control incompatible with our civil liberties. Would not an egalitarian society involve dictatorship?

Third, it is claimed, inequality is inevitable – either as a precondition of a successfully functioning society or as an inevitable consequence of social rule following.

Finally, systems of inequality are notoriously (or typically) stable. The presumed resentments generated by the knowledge that one occupies a particular subordinate position in a stratified society do not, as might be expected, always generate deep discontent and radical social change. On the contrary people adapt, often quite successfully, to the facts of inequality. In a 'nearly just' society, given a proper rationale for unequal distribution might not the demand for more equality be described more appropriately as mere envy – a destructive and non-moral response?

(vi)   Is equality desirable?

The argument that equality has no intrinsic merit has been developed by Robert Nozick in his influential book *Anarchy, State and Utopia*.[11] Nozick prefaces his argument by noting that egalitarians are not simply concerned with the distribution of goods and services but with their redistribution. They begin, that is, with the assumption that there is something wrong with all existing distributions. But, Nozick argues, why start from this arbitrary premiss? Surely it is more reasonable to see existing systems of distribution in a historical rather than a utopian perspective. In any case, he suggests, it is wildly inaccurate to talk of unequal distribution in society as if inequalities have arisen from a central source whose function is to dole out resources according to some specified criterion. He writes: 'We are not in the position of children who have been given portions of pie by someone who now makes last minute adjustments to rectify careless cutting.'[12]

The very conception of egalitarianism, then, seems to imply, at the best, paternalism or, at worst, dictatorship. But he argues no state has achieved this degree of control over the distributive process. What has happened is that the process of distribution is the consequence of the historically based decisions of countless generations of individuals on the basis of diverse criteria of entitlement. And it is from these empirical and historical origins that one should start.

Nozick defines the 'appropriation of unheld things' as 'holdings'.[13] Such 'holdings' would include property, both personal and corporate, and other less tangible social goods. Nozick argues that there is nothing necessarily or prima facie illegitimate in certain individuals or groups acquiring holdings at the expense of others provided they have acquired the holding in a just way and engage in transfer of holdings justly. Clearly I have no 'justified holding' if I steal or perpetrate a fraud to gain property. If I follow the rules, however, my entitlement is established and ought not to be questioned. As Nielsen neatly summarises the issue between Nozick and egalitarians, on Nozick's account:[14]

> Our maxim for justice should *not* be: 'Holdings ought to be equal unless there is a weighty moral reason why they ought to be unequal' . . . rather our maxim should be: 'People are entitled to keep whatever they happen to have unless there is a weighty moral reason why they ought to give it up.'

The burden of proof then has been shifted by Nozick on to the shoulders of the egalitarian who wishes to justify redistribution.

There are two questions which need to be addressed here. First, is the Formal Principle of Equality embraced by 'liberal' theorists and egalitarians alike but rejected by Nozick, arbitrary and non-historical? Second, is an egalitarian society necessarily committed to an abandonment of the notion of entitlement?

Many anti-egalitarians and anti-socialists commonly use the tactic of appeal to the particular, the concrete, and the actual rather than to the abstract, the theoretical and the general. These latter terms connote a utopian frame of mind according to critics and hence are viewed as wholly unrealistic. This cavalier attitude towards utopian thought is, in my view, misplaced. Of course, one should be deeply suspicious of blueprints for a utopian society. Nonetheless utopian ideas need not form the basis for a detailed construction of an ideal society. Utopianism may be viewed as the articulation of moral ideals which are, to use the jargon, 'deliberative' rather than 'verdictive'. That is, general, theoretical moral postulates serve to emphasise differing sets of moral considerations which might influence one in coming to a particular moral verdict. Thus the principles of freedom, as absence of constraint, and the principles of egalitarianism can be seen as embodying moral considerations which have to

66

be taken into account in reaching a moral verdict. Taken in isolation, neither principle can dictate a verdict – whether political or moral; rather they are used in the process of deliberation prior to making a particular decision. If one needs to make some particular judgment upon whether, for example, to place constraints upon or to abolish a system of private 'elite' schools, both principles draw attention to possibly competing prima facie moral requirements.

It is no criticism, then, to argue that egalitarianism makes reference to abstract principles. We all do this when we reflect seriously upon moral and political issues. The further question that Nozick raises, however, is why accept the formal principle of equality at all? Why should it be assumed that, prima facie, all people should be treated equally and given equal shares in the common stock?

To justify this principle would take us too far afield into one of the most fundamental problems in moral philosophy – the justification of high-level general principles. There is a sense, however, in which commitment to such principles does seem 'less arbitrary' than commitment to the prima facie value of existing states of affairs.

According to Nozick's view, the onus is upon the egalitarian to provide good reasons for justifying any form of redistribution of present 'holdings' within the particular society of which he is a member. Whether or not this is a 'private-property hugging view for which no rationale is evident', as Nielsen believes, there is clearly a sense in which such a demand is arbitrary. It is arbitrary in the sense that the general standard which one grants special status to is something like, 'Whatever is held is, prima facie, justifiably held.' But in specifying 'what is held' we are given an open class of social arrangements, customs and criteria of entitlement. In one society entitlement might be granted by inheritance through the male line, through the attribution of magical powers or in virtue of some perceived mystical ability. In another society entitlements might be based upon intelligence, hard work, initiative, enterprise and so forth. In other words, Nozick gives us no consistent rule according to which we may judge entitlements relatively independent of culture and social structure. His view comes close to a 'culturally relative' notion of 'just distribution'. And this is in essence arbitrary. How one interprets the notion of 'just entitlement' is dependent upon random historical accident.

Contrast this view with that of adherents to the Formal Principle of Equality which places the burden of justification upon those seeking to discriminate in the allocation of holdings. Here we have a clear rule which is widely rooted in our sense of fairness; the view that we have a natural right to be treated equally as humans – not in virtue of our birth, status or merit but in virtue of 'our capacity to make plans and give justice'.

We are inclined to express our sense of fairness by saying, 'No matter what society we live in or what social and historical forces moulded our lives we need to justify treating people differently.' Of course, over a very wide range in any given society there will be an almost unquestioned assumption that certain social virtues do in fact justify the unequal distribution of the common stock. But we expect these social virtues to be specified and argued for in particular cases. We are prepared, for example, to argue that the lower-paid should pay less tax because they are lower-paid and that the rich and powerful may 'deserve' greater reward in virtue of their 'greater social responsibility' and so forth. The point is that most of us believe that the tax system should bear equally upon all, other things being equal. And this is expressed at the abstract level in the Formal Principle of Equality.

This appeal to our moral intuitions is, of course, not decisive. Others may and will have contrary intuitions. But it surely establishes that the Principle of Equality is less arbitrary than a culturally relative principle of endorsing prima facie whatever is owned or 'held'? Let me put it this way. Which principle is more arbitrary – continue the series by adding 'two' successively $(2 + 4 + 6 + 8 \ldots)$ or continue the series with whatever happens to be the number of your and your neighbours' children $(2 + 1 + 4 + 0 + 1 \ldots)$.

Of course, if one just opts for saying, 'I take property rights to be morally fundamental and don't see that this is any more "arbitrary" than taking equality of consideration as a basic human right', then there is a certain sense in which further argument may be redundant. What I am arguing however is that the selection of property rights (whatever their justification and content) is on inspection more arbitrary than the choice of the rule of equal shares.

The second question, as I previously noted, concerns the view egalitarians take of entitlement. Must egalitarians dispense with the idea of 'just entitlement'? Obviously not! As Nielsen rightly comments notions of entitlement 'are most at home in situations where a person has mixed his labour and care with something say . . . built a house . . . or a family farm.' Radical egalitarians, suggests Nielsen, are not challenging entitlements of this type.[15]

> Socialists do not want to take people's homes or farms
> from them. The private property socialists seek to
> eliminate is private ownership and control of the major
> means of production . . . not private ownership of things
> like cars, houses, family farms, fishing boats and the
> like . . . It is the ownership and control of the major
> industries that is crucial.

In these latter areas 'entitlement', whether 'earned' by investment, takeover bid or the like is subsidiary to wider concerns for social equality. The egalitarian rule is something like: entitlement can only be justified if it can be shown that the holding of the particular property is consistent with the removal of the grosser forms of social inequity.

At this point I must add a caveat. The major reason for abolishing inequalities is that they operate as a constraint and hindrance upon people's desires. Egalitarianism is 'enabling'.

By removing the grosser forms of inequalities it seeks to give people the possibility of living fuller, more autonomous lives. Whether they choose to avail themselves of the greater opportunities given by a more equal society is however a further and different question. For those people in a dominant role in the society, however, equality may threaten liberty. Their liberties might be diminished by egalitarian measures. Under these circumstances they will, of course, appeal to 'entitlement'. In a democratic socialist society such appeals whether justified abstractly or not must be taken seriously. It is impossible to erect an egalitarian society overnight or even in three weeks! Citizens of a society whatever class they belong to have settled expectations upon which they have based their life plans. These plans ought not to be severely disrupted in the interests of promoting immediate equality. A perception of entitlement by a significant group of citizens, whether justified abstractly or not, must be treated with respect. This is not only true on the basis of the moral considerations adduced above but upon severely practical political grounds. Any society in which perceived entitlements are ridden over roughshod is likely to degenerate into open conflict or, as a response, into authoritarian state rule.

Egalitarianism is a question of the long haul. It involves a process of continuous, public persuasion and the tolerance of manifest setbacks to its aims. It needs to be pursued not with moral fervour but with calm, deliberate public argumentation and respect for minority rights – particularly the rights of those who may be required to make some sacrifice to achieve its long-term implementation.

In effect, what I have just written constitutes an answer to the second of the questions with which I began this section – does egalitarianism necessarily connote an authoritarian conception of politics? Is its implementation necessarily subversive of our civil liberties? The answer is clear. Egalitarianism properly conceived and properly argued for within the confines of accepted democratic procedures need imply no attenuation of basic liberties. This is not to say however that the pursuit of equality and the pursuit of individual liberty are necessarily compatible either! Both of these great deliberative moral principles must be brought to bear in coming to a verdict upon what is the optimal social policy to pursue in particular circumstances.

(vii)   Is inequality inevitable?

There are two broad sets of arguments designed to show that inequalities are necessary features of human social life. The first of these rests upon certain assumptions about human biology and psychology; the second maintains that social stratification is an ineliminable feature of any functioning society.

One of the oft-repeated arguments against socialism is that it is 'against human nature'. Look around you, so the argument goes, nowhere in the long history of mankind can we point to the existence of a genuine community of equals. Everywhere we see competition for scarce resources, for sexual dominance, for recognition, fame and fortune. And has not modern biology since Darwin demonstrated that competition functions to sustain and improve the species? Isn't there clear evidence of a 'natural pecking order' in a variety of animal communities? As humans, it is argued, we are members of the animal kingdom and subject to the laws of evolution which have resulted, at least for the time being, in the dominance of our species.

There are several strands to be distinguished in this popular hotch-potch of argument and assertion. The first thing to note is that the very idea of 'human nature' is ambiguous. Much of what we assume to be 'natural to man' is the product of our restricted upbringing and social consciousness. What is 'natural' to a prairie farmer from Saskatchewan is not necessarily 'natural' to a Sudanese peasant or an East German industrial worker. Anthropologists have consistently argued that concepts of what is 'natural to man' are relative to culture'. Different languages, it is suggested, embody totally dissimilar world views in which we are, so to speak, imprisoned. Even our concepts of space and time, it is suggested, are taken-for-granted assumptions which are virtually unchallengeable within our own cultural and social milieu. There may be a fundamental sense in which we are locked into our own conceptions and unable fully to understand the world view of an Inuit, for example, from our perspective as members of industrial European or North American societies.

Although the doctrine of 'cultural relativism' is both overstated and ultimately unsustainable it contains much truth. Clearly it requires great imagination and effort to transcend our own world-view. Most of us simply do not have the information available on other cultures to make proper comparisons and judgments. We are too busy in living within our own 'paramount reality' – the day-to-day demands of our 'ordinary' life which require us to respond and act on assumptions which work for us here and now. It is only, perhaps, the fortunate leisured few who are privileged to reflect in detail upon the disparities of human social organisation and values.

What most of us take to be 'natural', 'ain't necessarily so!' We may feel that incentives and rewards are necessary to sustain an efficient level of work; that men will necessarily strive for power and status and that human wants are limitless. But these assumptions may be socially derived. Were we to live in a culture where cooperation and not competition were the norm our conception of human nature might be fundamentally different.

Even allowing for 'historical evidence' against the possibility of an egalitarian society we cannot argue that egalitarianism is necessarily a utopian dream. It might be, as Kai Nielsen suggests, that an egalitarian society can only emerge under conditions of 'moderate abundance' with concomitant changes in some of our fundamental social attitudes. And surely one cannot argue that the development of a rational technology which consistently works both to increase production and to protect and conserve the natural environment is inconceivable?

Be that as it may, isn't there some force in the argument that there must be certain general and universal features of human nature? After all, we are all members of the same species occupying the same position within the evolutionary process and subject to the same laws of natural selection and biological and genetic development. This, of course, cannot be denied. The problem is to separate and distinguish those elements of our 'common humanity' which can be traced to 'biological' as against 'social and cultural' factors. Many sociobiologists, for example, have linked human patterns of aggression, sexual behaviour, family relationships and even so-called 'altruism' to animal and insect behaviour. The fundamental mechanism linking us all to the rest of the animal world, it has been asserted, is the idea of the 'selfish gene'. In all animals, it is argued, there is an innate tendency for the gene to seek to propagate itself and to multiply. This may be illustrated, it is suggested, by the universal tendency in animal and human life to favour one's kin over 'strangers'. Special preference is given to close relations since they carry a high percentage of the parent organisms' genetic endowment. According to this model patterns of animal behaviour are fundamentally characterised by competition amongst and between species. Social cooperation is always and everywhere a form of self-interested (or gene-interested) behaviour.

The findings of biologists on insect and bird communities have been extrapolated to human societies. Thus we find sociobiology being used to defend 'competitive capitalism', for example, and National Front 'theoreticians' have also seized upon sociobiology in order to defend racialism.

Of course, sociobiology is not necessarily linked to the defence of right-wing or racialist views but its stress upon the

ultimate significance of the genetic causes of human behaviour certainly lends itself to these kinds of interpretations.

What is more important, however, is that sociobiologists
make a number of assumptions which are unwarranted.
They simply assume that one can make extrapolations from
insect and bird behaviour to comparable-looking human
behaviour. What they ignore, of course, is the extent to
which human behaviour is shaped by culture – that complex
set of expectations, values, rules and intentions which
characterise a human community as distinct from a colony of
bees, for example. Furthermore, many biologists have
characterised the sociobiologists' idea of a discrete gene
which more or less directly controls behaviour as naive.
The gene is apparently much more complex than the socio-
biologist has imagined. Also lacking is an account of the
meditation processes between the gene and behaviour. We do
not know precisely by what mechanisms the gene affects the
complex behaviour of humans. What we can say is that there
is certainly a genetic component to all human behaviour but
how that component relates to other social and cultural
factors is impossible to assess. Even to distinguish genetic
from cultural components of behaviour is extraordinarily
difficult – except in very simple cases like eye-colour or the
existence of the disease called sickle-cell anaemia for
example.

The upshot of all this is that sociobiological explanations of
human behaviour are at present largely speculative.

Sociobiologists have no well-grounded view of human
nature and, what is more, cannot logically derive any clear
implications for political and social behaviour from their
doctrines.

It may be suggested, however, that we do not need to
evaluate the technicalities of sociobiology in order to assert
the inevitability of hierarchy. Surely some people are 'naturally' more intelligent, hard-working and emotionally well-
balanced than others and isn't this fact reflected to a certain

extent in all systems of social stratification? How can it be that socialists argue for equality of ranking in society where there are obvious natural differences in rank between people?

This kind of argument has a long history. Aristotle, for example, justified the existence of social inequalities on just this basis. His idea, crudely speaking, was that inborn character, 'breeding' and ability would be reflected in a justly ordered hierarchical society. On this view, individuals are, as a matter of fact, socially differentiated and in virtue of our estimate of their 'natural' abilities we come to endorse or to criticise the prevailing system of social stratification. Suppose, to take a simplified example, we believe in the idea of a meritocracy – the view that those who demonstrate a high degree of 'IQ + effort' ought to be better rewarded than others. Our ideal stratification system would be one in which the most intelligent and hard-working would occupy the top rungs of the ladder and those less well endowed with these attributes the lower rungs. Upon this basis we might approve or disapprove of the actual inequalities in particular societies. We might grade societies according to the degree to which they satisfied this criterion for the justification of inequalities.

What this view ignores, however, is that the fact of social differentiation in itself carries no weight in the justification of inequalities. Egalitarians are strong defenders of the desirability of maintaining social differences based upon similarity of interests, values or tastes. What is crucial is that those who argue for a link between differences, whether in temperament, skin colour or whatever, and the justification of inequalities, assume that certain social differences have a special value for the society. That is, there can be no direct inference from the fact of human differences to the desirability that these differences be reflected in a system of social hierarchy without the intervention of a value-premiss. Why, that is, should we prefer differentially to reward 'IQ + effort' rather than 'gentleness', height, hair colour or some other 'natural' attribute? Only because we place a special value on certain human attributes rather than upon others. There can be, then, no direct unmediated link between the 'natural' and the 'social'.

There is, of course, the further question often suppressed in arguments of the kind just discussed, that it is necessary to reward socially those people possessing valued attributes. Egalitarians question this assumption. They would argue that it is less a question of granting special privileges to those of 'superior ability' than of allowing full rein to the autonomous development of all human abilities consistent with the welfare of all.

(viii) The argument from 'incentives'

Recent sociological defences of inequality have concentrated upon the necessity to reward valued characteristics in the interests of maintaining an efficient society. Inequality is seen as a 'functional prerequisite' of all possible societies. This is simply a reiteration of the old 'incentives' argument in sociological disguise. The view is that the 'frictionless' allocation of social positions necessitates rewarding those most fitted to fill them. The assumption is that without such rewards able individuals will choose other less arduous and responsible pursuits thus tending to undermine optimum efficiency. There is a further assumption that all relatively 'successful' or 'persisting' societies have mechanisms which encourage those best fitted to occupy 'functionally important' social roles. This conception of social hierarchy dates back to Plato with his conception of 'arête', or excellence in function, as the single most important feature of a just state.

It scarcely needs commenting, however, that in no society is it self-evident that the greatest rewards go to those most qualified and competent to occupy 'key positions'. In any case it is a matter of moral and political dispute as to which 'roles' are 'key' or 'functional' and not just a question of sociological description. Of course, in the absence of mechanisms for the recruitment of individuals to socially important roles, societies would not function to the maximum benefit of all and might even disintegrate. But this fact alone does not entail that we need a system of unequal rewards to guarantee efficiency. There might be other ways – forced labour, an appeal to civic duty and so forth – which might achieve the same end. What the so-called 'structural-functionalist' sociologists seem to be arguing is that inequalities are necessary in any society, and in virtue of that fact, are either desirable or a 'necessary evil' (whatever that phrase means). Egalitarians would contest the former claim thus denying the logical link to the latter.

A more ambitious and interesting argument for the inevitability of inequality is that proposed by Professor Ralf Dahrendorf who seeks to deduce the idea of inequality from the very concept of society. He argues that there could not logically be a 'republic of equals' in the sense understood by radical egalitarians.

Dahrendorf's argument runs as follows. All societies are 'moral communities' and as such need to establish rules to which sanctions are attached prescribing various types of conformity and proscribing types of non-conformity. These rules will be promulgated in the law of the land but they are not confined to legal rules. For those who conform, Dahrendorf implies, there will of necessity be social rewards; for those who deviate there will be social punishments. These non-legal rewards and punishments will take the form of inequalities of status and class position. Conformity to the prevailing norms will bring high status; non-conformity lower status. As he puts it:[16]

> Because there are norms and because sanctions are necessary to enforce conformity . . . there has to be inequality of rank amongst men.

Here the force of 'has to be' is logical not simply empirical.

Dahrendorf is usually a perceptive and acute social analyst but here the argument seems unusually weak. As Steven Lukes has pointed out:[17]

Dahrendorf slides unaccountably from the undoubted truth that within groups norms are enforced which discriminate against certain persons and positions . . . to the *unsupported* claim that within society as a whole a system of inequality is inevitable.

The reason why Dahrendorf commits this logical howler is not difficult to understand. Dahrendorf, as a committed 'liberal' and ex-member of the German Free Democratic Party, is strongly opposed both to the 'structural function-alist' view of a consensus-based harmonious society and to what he conceives of as utopian Marxist notions of a classless (and hence conflict-free) society. In all historical or existing societies inequality, he argues, is a logical consequence of 'real' rather than utopian social structures. Inequality, he asserts, is often an evil but its existence guarantees the possi-bility of social change and historical development. Inequali-ties symbolise for him the necessary clash of values between conformists and deviants in a society.

The presence of inequalities guarantees the 'non-utopian' nature of societies in general as opposed to entirely visionary conceptions dreamed of by the apostles of a New Order whether of the political right or left.

But even the weaker claim that inequalities are a necessary feature of democratic (or 'pluralist') societies cannot be main-tained. It is certainly not the case that conformity to estab-lished opinion is always rewarded socially in a democracy. Indeed a conformist or deferential attitude towards authority on the part of the working classes may actually increase their deprivation. To defer to established values is often an invita-tion to participate in one's own social devaluation rather than in the promotion of one's status.

No serious egalitarian entertains a conception of a conflict-free society. The question is whether social conflict is necessarily associated with the existence of inequalities? Of course where inequalities exist conflict may occur. But the contrary is not necessarily true. Social conflict and differences of interest are possible and desirable in an egalitarian society. Inequalities may be a source of conflict, conflict is not necessarily a source of inequality.

(ix)   Why are systems of inequality relatively stable?

One serious impediment to the implementation of egalitarian policies is that stratification systems are resistant to change. This is quite surprising especially where wide inequalities exist in politically democratic societies. Of course in authoritarian states there is not much of a sociological puzzle about why wide disparities of class and status persist. In such societies the citizenry are unable to express grievances adequately. Their lives are dominated by the blatant use of political and military power to enforce their masters' will.

The use of power, in perhaps a more subtle form, is not unknown in more democratic societies. Perhaps it is still the most important element in the maintenance of hierarchical structures. Everything turns, however, upon a difference in degree. In a Stalinist or Nazi state or in present-day South Africa or Chile serious challenges to ruling groups may be met with imprisonment, torture, arbitrary arrest, harassment or exile. In democratic societies this is clearly less likely to occur. Where power is abused the power holders are accountable to the public and although such accountability does not always square in practice with the ideal democratic model the idea does have genuine application. All is not mere 'bougeois ideology'!

The sociological puzzle is that all stratification systems seem in principle to be potentially explosive. One would expect that those at the top of any system of gross inequalities would be satisfied with their position whilst those at the bottom would be deeply resentful and hostile. These attitudes would generally be expected to foster, if not revolution, then radical fervour. This, however, does not seem to be the case.

From a Marxist perspective, given an attachment to the historical necessity of class polarisation, the position of the unenlightened or 'falsely conscious' working class in capitalist societies has been equally disturbing. For Marxists what has to be postulated is a cunning and subtle 'conspiracy' on the part of the ruling class to manipulate the consciousness of the proletarian. A whole academic and propaganda industry is now devoted to the question of why the working class in the industrial West is ignorant of its true historical role.

Maybe something of value will emerge from this. The problem is, however, that the question of the stability of hierarchy is posed within a theoretical framework in which certain answers are already excluded. The 'proletarian' is viewed essentially either as a personification of class consciousness – a true representative of the 'class-for-itself' – or as a puppet in the hands of the manipulative ruling class. Answers to the question of how members of the working class feel about their position have already been evaluated. There is a 'right' and 'wrong' response – and the 'wrong' response naturally requires special, often *ad hoc*, explanation.

Now it may be true that the reluctance of the British (or North American) working class to commit themselves to a party of the radical left is partially a product of their direct suppression or manipulation but to many democratic socialists this seems to be neither a particularly plausible nor exhaustive answer. It requires no great stretch of the imagination to see that the British working class could, if it so wished, ensure the near permanent rule of a left-wing non-Communist Labour government. The reasons why it does not do so may be complex but most of the analysis undertaken takes for granted that the working class suffer from a high degree of felt deprivation. That is, many analysts work with the simple psychological model that intensity of felt deprivation correlates closely with position in the hierarchy.

In 1966 this assumption was challenged by W.G. Runciman in his book *Relative Deprivation and Social Justice*.[18] As far as I am aware the book is still in print (1984), which attests to its significance. In general, however, the left has been suspicious of Runciman's main thesis. Charges have been levelled that his work is naively empirical, over-psychological and anti-socialist. I want to redress the balance. It seems to me that Runciman's analysis fosters a greater understanding of the stability of class hierarchy in the West. It is not, I believe, incompatible with socialism or radical egalitarianism. It is a study which gives due weight to the opinions and attitudes of the working class without devaluing their response in advance on theoretical grounds. It does not claim to give an exhaustive account of why stratification systems are resistant to alteration but it does offer a perspective which is wholly absent from traditional Marxist interpretations. What then has Runciman to say?

Runciman seeks to explain the apparent paradox that people's attitudes to objective social inequalities seldom correlate strictly with the facts of their own position. On the common sense assumption that intense resentment will be generated in those suffering from inequalities of class and status one would expect a high degree of political activism and radical fervour on the part of the working class. This 'commonsense assumption', however, is valid only where the member of the working class has a reasonably accurate perception of the extent of inequality; where they conceive themselves as being equal in desert or merit to those in superior positions and where they have the power to translate their feelings into political action.

In fact, Runciman argues, in mid-twentieth century British society working class men and women appear to restrict themselves to comparative judgments across a very narrow range of class or status positions. In evaluating inequality, that is, they tend to make comparisons only to 'those in the same boat as themselves'. Comparative reference to other groups seems as limited, according to Runciman, as it is typically in wage negotiations. Manual workers do not normally take as their economic 'reference-group' the occupational category of High Court judges nor do schoolteachers habitually compare their salaries and working conditions to those of company directors in large business organisations. As a consequence, Runciman argues, individuals or groups low in the hierarchical scale experience not the full range of resentment, anger and sense of injustice which would be generated by comparisons across the hierarchical board as it were but only 'relative deprivation'. The narrower the range of reference the less intense and widespread would be feelings of deprivation.

The subjective state of relative deprivation arises, Runciman suggests, from the fact that 'people's attitudes, aspirations and grievances depend largely upon the frame of reference within which they are conceived'. For some groups certain comparisons are not felt to be 'feasible' and the consequence is that low-status groups may be relatively content with limited gains in comparison with groups slightly above them in the class system. Such limited gains may, however, be trivial in the context of the very wide discrepancies between the dominant and subordinate classes.

Runciman's book is full of documented contemporary and historical examples of the way in which restriction of reference groups plays an important role in the dampening down of objectively justifiable resentment, and hence of political action, on the part of the underprivileged. One of the most illuminating and persuasive of his examples concerns the response during the 1930s to proposed changes in unemployment relief. The government of the day sought to centralise and regulate the payment of unemployment benefit through passage of the Unemployment Act of 1934. The Act was designed to penalise local authorities such as Poplar, West

Ham and Chester-le-Street who were deemed to be 'overspending' on unemployment relief and to raise the standards for other 'underspending' local authorities. As Runciman observes:[19]

> On the appointed day, January 7th, *The Times'* first editorial smugly declared that 'Everything points to the prospect that 1935 will be a distinctly happier year for most of those who, in spite of the industrial recovery, will not be able to find work'.

What actually happened was that the vast majority of recipients of unemployment relief had their benefits cut. The extent and volume of the protest was, by English standards, spectacular. Opposition was vocal, pressure intense and the government was forced into a conciliatory, even apologetic, position. Eventually, a standstill order was issued on 5 February and 'increases were allowed to stand but the reductions annulled.'

Such a blaze of political agitation over what was after all a 'trivial' further deprivation viewed in the light of the glaring inequalities of class and status is, on the surface, difficult to understand. Why was it that such a heightened political awareness was not continuously directed towards the radical amelioration of working class distress? Runciman's answer is to suggest that 'frustrated expectations are less readily tolerable than consistent hardship'. Feelings of relative deprivation, that is, are heightened when the populace at large has been encouraged to feel that improvements in their condition of life are feasible. In the absence of these expectations people often adjust to hardship as they would to the existence of some natural, physical law. In the case cited politicians and public alike reacted to the worsening of a situation they had been led to believe was capable of improvement even though in the wider context such an improvement would be of little benefit to the unemployed or to the working class generally.

In order further to illustrate Runciman's contention that choice of 'reference-group' is significant in accounting for the relative stability of social hierarchy let us consider a hypothetical contemporary case.

Imagine the case of James Robinson, a married, 50-year-old, skilled manual worker in a so-called 'high-tech' industry. Let us assume that he, rightly or wrongly, supposes his job to be relatively secure. He lives in a small semi-detached house in a suburban area of a northern industrial city, earns slightly above the national average wage and owns outright a second-hand car. How might one characterise his political attitudes?

One might surmise him to be tolerably content with his lot. In comparison with his friends and workmates who may be unemployed, carless or live in local council houses he may even consider himself to be lucky. His political allegiance will probably be to the Labour Party and the trade union movement but he is on the whole unlikely to be a political or trade union activist. He is likely to be opposed to 'extremism' and suspicious of the 'Labour left.'

Assuming that this portrayal is typical of many members of the British working class, as seems likely upon Runciman's empirical evidence and upon the evidence of other survey material, we may characterise Mr Robinson as having a low degree of relative deprivation, as restricting his range of comparative reference to within the working class and as having a minor commitment to socialist policies.

But this characterisation is not a full explanation of Mr Robinson's attitudes for it leaves open the question of why there is this self-imposed restriction on his range of comparative reference. Is it that such a man is simply 'falsely conscious' of his own position or is there more to it? Are his views compatible with a proper realisation of the extent of inequalities in British society?

Of course, one possible explanation of such attitudes and feelings is that the man is plainly ignorant of the nature of the

British class structure or, if not wholly ignorant, then mis-informed and possibly 'deferential' to his class superiors. It is more likely, however, that his attitudes are a response to a very full realisation of class inequality. They may be a re-sponse both to his perception of the stability of class hier-archy and a psychological defence against the continuous stress involved in maintaining a high level of demand, ex-pectation and resentment.

Recent studies have shown that the working class have a view of the social structure as hostile to their interests in contrast to the sentiments of middle class professional groups, for example. Any success is seen as an overcoming of barriers rather than as a normally realisable expectation. If this is generally true then it is possible to argue for the accommodation of low levels of relative deprivation and a genuine appreciation of the extent of inequality. What a restriction of comparative reference may involve is an adapt-ive response to the realities of power. Members of the work-ing class may very properly conceive of the social structure as hostile and relatively entrenched. In such circumstances restriction of comparative reference cannot be construed as 'false consciousness' but as an intelligent adaptation to social reality. Of course such an adaptation may fall short of what committed socialists require from the working class but a political movement which bases its hopes upon what ought to be felt rather than what *is* felt is at a distinct disadvantage.

The range of comparative reference of the working class can, of course, be extended. As Runciman points out, post-war periods are often a time of radical social change. During war appeals are made to national rather than class sentiment; traditional occupational barriers are broken down and wages are often higher than in peacetime. Perhaps as important are economic shifts in which people's expectations may rise sharply or conversely may be severely and continuously denied. What Runciman calls 'the receipt of news' is also important. The more sources of information about 'how the other half live' the more the likelihood, other things being equal, that pressure will mount for political change.

What is most important for the 'destabilisation' of hierarchy, however, is to convince people that proposals for change are feasible. Once individuals or groups come to see that the class structure is not totally entrenched their understandable defensive responses may be modified. Every successful implementation of egalitarian measures may serve to fuel the next. This is not merely because a particular measure may be successful but because its success can materially alter the perceptions of the social world on the part of those forced into subordinate positions. Class authority, successfully challenged, becomes less authoritative, less likely to be conceived of as either legitimate or unalterable.

One hears a great deal, especially in Marxist circles, of the necessity to 'educate the working class'. Such sentiments are patronising and are rightly resisted by actual members of the working class as distinct from their self-appointed 'vanguard'. The working class as a whole do not stand in need of political education; what they need is to be convinced that their political participation, which may involve some personal sacrifice, has a realistic chance of altering the structure and extent of present inequalities. Vulgar imputation of 'false consciousness' does nothing to further this end.

(x) Does equality imply fraternity?

The idea of fraternity is metaphorical. It extends the notion of brotherhood within the community of the family to other groups – class, nation and mankind. There is a literal sense, of course, in which we cannot be fraternal with others. The plain fact is that strangers are not our brothers; nor can we always transpose our private relationships into the public arena. Much of the most significant, and trivial, aspects of social life depend upon our treating others 'in role' – as postmen, teachers, grocers, booking clerks and the like. One cannot always be exposed to 'the common humanity in others' when buying a jar of marmalade or an 'away-day' return to Basingstoke!

What the metaphor of fraternity draws attention to is that labelling others must be seen merely as a question of social convenience. It acts, to quote Bernard Williams, as a 're-minder' that we ought not, morally speaking, to treat people as objects on the basis of their more or less accidental occupational status but upon their character as persons.

That the appellations 'brother' and 'comrade' are habitual forms of address within the Labour movement is no accident. The essential component of both is a denial of the significance of hierarchy and an assertion of communal interest. Comradeship is only possible between equals – not necessarily 'status-equals', but where there is equality of respect grounded in notions of human worth and integrity.

The idea of fraternity, however, has a number of more loosely knit connotations deriving from the notion of a family community. Not only do we treat our brothers and sisters as persons 'in their own right' rather than as agents of another's will – we love them. That is, our responses to them are not conditioned by their desert or merit. We love them for 'what they are' – warts and all. Love, in an ideal family community, engenders loyalty and mutual help. Our obligations to our kin are not contractual. A family bound together only by legal ties is a degenerate form of community. Our obligations seem to arise 'naturally' out of our common parentage and from our shared experience of living together. Family relationships depend upon cooperation rather than conflict; love rather than 'rights'.

Members of a family are, of course, also citizens and where communal ties disintegrate appeals may be made to wider social rules to enforce obligations. In general, however, our sense of love and obligation to brothers and sisters is of a different kind to our obligations towards society. What the metaphor of 'fraternity' stresses is the moral desirability of the transfer of these attitudes, where possible, to all social relations.

It is important to note that the appeal to fraternity is distinguishable from treating the family as a model of existing or possible societies. It is not that our obligations to the state or wider society are, or ought to be, conceived of in precisely similar terms to that of the family. Rather the argument is that the virtues of loyalty, cooperation, mutual help and so on could, with profit, govern our dealings with others in general rather than with our kin in particular. What the idea of fraternity insists upon is the notion that 'structural change' must be associated with changes in social attitudes.

How is fraternity then related to equality? Clearly in one aspect they are the same. Both insist upon the moral irrelevance of hierarchy and social status; both insist upon equality of respect. But here the similarity ends. The idea of equality is enabling. It does not, however, define or dictate which forms of life or which set of social attitudes are desirable once the burdens of inequality are removed. An egalitarian society allows people to pursue their wants, provided these wants are compatible with the interests of others. It does not necessarily require a change of attitude but rather a change in behaviour. Of course, as a matter of fact, changes in attitude and behaviour may be mutually reinforcing. If I try to develop feelings of loyalty towards and love for my fellow men and women it is likely that my behaviour will exemplify this. If I consistently seek to promote the good in my behaviour it is likely that my attitudes and feelings will change. But this mutual relationship is not a necessary one. It is perfectly conceivable that one may be temperamentally highly competitive, for example, and yet seek to restrain that competitiveness where it issues in harm to others. There is much to be said for the view that socialism is not about attitudes of cooperation, non-contractual obligation, loyalty and the like but about behaviour.

This is one of the reasons why I feel unhappy about Nielsen's view that changes in attitude may be a prerequisite of the transition to a socialist society. It does seem to me to be 'wholly utopian' to require of us that we adopt a fraternal attitude towards others at a precondition of building an egalitarian society. Nielsen realistically assumes that in a society where there is still scarcity of resources competitive attitudes will be sustained. Only where there is 'moderate abundance', he suggests, will the possibility of an egalitarian society be realisable.

The trouble here is that the two criteria of 'moderate abundance' and 'change in attitude' make the idea of egalitarian society seem impossibly remote. It is surely asking too much of individuals or groups to change deeply entrenched individualist attitudes in the way he suggests. Indeed, I would argue, it is positively undesirable to insist upon such changes.

Whether it be a fact of 'nature' or of our particular culture, the notion of the individuated self is central to our conception of the world. We see the world through our eyes; we are interested primarily in our needs, our satisfactions and our projects. The whole notion of a morally autonomous person, rather than one swayed by the normative pressure of his peers, depends upon us holding fast to the idea of the integrity of the individual. In an egalitarian society individual civil liberty must be protected. We need the social space to develop differences, even eccentricities, in our ways of life and in our attitudes.

Let me speak personally, for a moment. I do not consider myself a 'cooperative' person. I dislike large social gatherings (football matches and parties excepted); I abhor academic conferences preferring to work on my own from books and through personal discussion with others; I seek vigorously to pursue my own interests and expect other people to pursue theirs; I am generally competitive and intellectually critical; I object strongly to hierarchy, blind loyalty to institutions or dogmas and to any form of social pressure to conform to this or that set of social rules. I do not think that my attitudes are eccentric or undesirable and I certainly do not wish to (and probably could not) change them markedly.

I am, however, prepared to accept constraints upon the realisation of my interests in the interests of others. Furthermore, my own steady conception of what is in my interest and of my own sense of personal identity strengthens rather than weakens my concern for the interest of others. Feeling as I do it takes little imagination to sympathise with those who are frustrated in the realisation of their wants by outmoded and repressive hierarchies or by interferences with their civil or personal liberties. I cannot love my fellow men nor can I think of them in the way I think of my brother. What I do see, however, is the prospect that life for all could be mightily improved by safeguarding liberty, dismantling the barriers of class and status and generating a greater sense of autonomy and control for all.

This example, though personal and perhaps egotistical, is illustrative of a wider concern. One needs to distinguish two senses of the term 'individualism'. Egoistic individualism which is careless of others' liberties and welfare and which is sanctioned and encouraged by laissez-faire and monopoly capitalism is morally to be deplored not as an attitude-in-itself but because it is associated with a social and economic system which constrains and damages human dignity and liberty. The sense of individualism which marks off a person as morally responsible for his acts, which asserts that his interests should be protected and consulted and which incorporates a demand for equality of respect is a radically different conception.

The idea of fraternity is deeply ambivalent with respect to individualism in this latter sense. Where the emphasis is upon equality of respect for persons there is no inherent conflict; where the accent is upon seeking to replace individualist conceptions with communal and cooperative attitudes towards social organisation there is the possibility of dispute and misunderstanding. It may well be that notions of non-contractual obligation, cooperation and community spirit will be enhanced in an egalitarian society but they cannot and should not be mandatory for all socialists. Egalitarianism, strictly defined, is compatible both with individualist and cooperative temperaments and attitudes. Egalitarians ought not to aim at the development of collective consciousness; rather cooperation must be seen as a way of enhancing the life of each citizen. One may hold that poverty and hierarchy are social ills not upon the basis of commitment to an ideal of social cooperation but upon a secure and settled conception of the significance of individual identity.

3 Conclusion: morality and socialism

'The undiscussed life is not worth living.'

SOCRATES

(i) Morality: substantive, procedural and critical

The word 'moral' (or 'ethical') may be used in two distinct ways. In one sense when I attach the word to acts or to persons I am showing approval of them. I might, for example, express my approval of some piece of legislation by saying that it was morally right. The second use of the word 'moral' does not, however, necessarily carry this positive sense of approval. I may describe whole systems of belief and action as 'moral', even if I disapprove of them strongly. I might say, for example, that I disapproved of the moral code of the military.

In other words the two different senses of the word 'moral' are used to mark a distinction between those sets of beliefs or principles which the speaker or writer holds to be, in some sense, morally 'correct' or desirable and those beliefs or principles which might conceivably count as being within the realm of moral discourse. We might say, for example, that the principle 'Don't harm others gratuitously' was a moral principle in both senses of the word whereas 'Be loyal to those superior in rank' might qualify in one sense only.

I intend to use the distinction 'procedural/substantive' to mark the difference then between what is common to all possible ethical systems – what marks them off, say, from the physical sciences or mathematics – and what principles may be conceived differently within ethics. One may clearly oppose a 'conservative morality' yet be unwilling to deny that it falls within the bounds of that idea. Let me explain further.

Suppose three people meet to discuss their ethical values – a socialist, a conservative and another of no clearly defined political views. The socialist may argue for optimising the application of the principles of freedom and equality; the conservative may defend authority and hierarchy. Both of these positions are in principle defensible; both lie within the ambit of rational moral debate. Suppose, however, the third individual simply says that he has in his possession a computer which through the operation of some as yet improperly understood mechanism has developed a 'moral sense'. This moral sense is exhibited through its giving answers to the question 'What ought I (or we) to do?' in the form of 'categorical imperatives' which although they are formulated in ordinary language bear little relation to what most of us 'ordinarily' understand by morality. Suppose the computer responds to the questions put to it by repeating in varying order the following answers:

(1) 'Sit down and contemplate your navel.'
(2) 'Eat sausages on Tuesday.'
(3) 'Never play cricket wearing pyjamas.'
(4) 'Salute your betters.'

and crucially

(5) 'Never criticise.'

The sheer silliness of these answers may seem wholly to disqualify them as possible moral principles; but this is not so. Rules embodying deference to one's superiors, dietary regulation, ritual dressing and mysticism have certainly been considered to fall within the range of what the idea of morality encompasses. What appears to disqualify this version of 'computer-based morality' is that the 'advice' generated by the computer seems random, unreasoned and more importantly specifically prohibits any form of criticism of its own arbitrary dictates.

It is just this element – the permanent possibility of criticism of moral principles – which seems to me to characterise all possible moral points of view. In entering the moral arena one necessarily enters into the realm of debate. That this is so can be demonstrated most persuasively by considering the function of moral language.

The point of moral discourse, unlike that of discourse in the natural sciences, is to provide answers to the question 'What ought I (or others) to do?'

It might be argued, however, that there are other ways of determining answers to this question. For example, the law instructs us in what we ought to do over a wide range of our behaviour. Legal discourse, that is, incorporates a 'legal ought' whose authority rests upon common and statute law as properly promulgated and endorsed and reflected in court decisions. Criticism of particular laws or particular legal decisions within a strictly legal context centres around concepts such as 'validity' and 'legitimation' not typically those of justice and morality. Thus the question 'Why ought I to do X?' is answered by the statement 'Because the law requires it.' The further question 'Why ought I to obey the law?' can only be taken to mean in a legal context 'How do I identify valid laws?' and now 'How am I to tell if the laws are just?'

Nevertheless it is obvious that questions as to the justice of laws need to be raised. Is civil disobedience ever justified? If so, under what circumstances and what form of government? Only a rigid and narrow legalist would assert that these questions were capable of being answered negatively as a matter of course. Indeed changes in our legal system depend upon us having a language available in which we may challenge the justice of any particular law.

What is true for the law is true on the personal level. Answers to the question 'What ought I to do?' are frequently answered in purely prudential terms – that is, 'Do what is in your best interest.' Typically a response to the question 'Should I invest five hundred pounds in Krugerrands?' would be 'Certainly, if your conscience can live with it without causing you too much distress and if you think gold coins are the best possible investment.' Here again, however, we might want to challenge the restriction of scope, in the example cited, to merely self-interested considerations. We might want to point to the fact that indirectly one was helping to bolster the South African Government's repressive and racialist policies and so forth.

Exactly the same arguments apply to purely political judgments made on the grounds of expediency or national interest. Once again in order to challenge a purely political decision as 'cynical' or 'heedless of others' interest' we cannot be confined to the language of politics alone. We require a discourse whose point is to enable us to challenge the restriction of scope of possible considerations to factors such as the law, self- or national interest or power. This is precisely what moral language is.

Moral language embodies the 'permanent possibility of criticism'. That is, it enables us, should we so wish, to criticise our own actions and the actions of others by pointing to sets of relevant considerations other than those appealed to by the lawyer, politician or other agent of social control. Socially defined roles notoriously narrow people's vision and restrict the scope of their judgments. Moral language allows for this ubiquitous tendency to be challenged. It serves the purpose of rational human agents who need *a language which permits the permanent possibility of critical assessment of social rules*.

What I am arguing here is that the maxim 'Never criticise' could not conceivably function as a distinctively moral postulate. This is not because I approve of critical debate (although, of course, I do) but because adoption of such a principle would negate the whole point of morality. One could not proceed beyond the first dogmatic answer 'Do this' to the question 'What ought I to do?'

The critical procedural principle which lies at the heart of moral language does not necessarily imply a substantive liberal 'open' morality. It is quite possible to envisage a highly authoritarian moral system which was compatible with the 'permanent possibility of criticism'. One might, for example, imagine a society ruled by an elite whose judgment was so valued by the populace at large that its orders were habitually obeyed even although they were highly paternalist. Under this system social rules might come to be conceived of as something akin to 'sacred' pronouncements in the sense that they were never or very rarely in fact criticised. But what is definitive of morality is the permanent possibility of criticism not the permanent presence of criticism. If it could be shown that the members and rulers of the society in question were always prepared seriously to listen to criticism and to allow it to influence their judgments then, no matter how 'revered' social rules were to become there would be clear evidence of the existence of a distinctively moral community. This would be true even if we regarded their rules as (substantively) morally wrong.

Of course in the 'real' world as distinct from that of constructed philosophical examples lack of positive evidence of criticism of social rules is often indicative of authoritarian, repressive or barbarous regimes for whom the philosophical considerations adduced here would have no meaning or application. The point I am making however is that in all societies people feel the need to criticise existing social rules and to find new considerations relevant in arguing for their change or modification. Where this procedure occurs people become engaged in distinctively moral argument.

The characterisation I have given of moral discourse might be thought to involve endless theorising and debate – the sort of mutual navel gazing engaged in by earnest and theoretical 'shock-headed Marxists chewing polysyllables'.[1] This is not so. For, of course, the point of moral discourse is to provide a rationale for acting. Without acting in the world moral debate is rendered redundant or, better perhaps, becomes a rather fascinating intellectual game. But why engage in moral philosophising anyway if the point is not to interpret the world but to change it?

The short answer is that you cannot or ought not to try to change the world without trying to understand the rationale for existing practices. The longer answer would involve saying why it is important to articulate the features of a distinctively human way of life which could in principle be understood cross-culturally. But perhaps the most appropriate response to this fundamental question is to point out that moral appraisal and moral 'theorising' are common human pursuits and that most people are not content with merely *ad hoc* or *ad hominem* moral strictures and advice. We want ourselves and others to be morally consistent. We want to generate from our own experience of moral disagreements and perplexities some reasonably systematic or coherent framework within which we can accommodate and defend our personal and our political judgments.

(ii)   The presumption of freedom and equality

Socialism is not a religion or at any rate it ought not to be regarded as one. Socialist politics aims not at making people better but rather removing burdens from them. Many democratic socialists would not agree. They would suggest, if not insist, that fraternalism, cooperation and altruism are necessary features of any socialist society worthy of the name. How, they might inquire, can a socialist society be created and sustained if self-interest and individualism remain as the central motivations of its citizens? What lies behind this view is the optimistic conception of human nature as essentially moulded by social and economic practices. Remove the distortions imposed by capitalism, so the argument runs, and there will be a necessary inward transformation of people from 'alienated' and 'atomistic' units into cooperative, 'sharing' members of the body-politic.

To attach the possibility of achieving socialism to such a naive and unverifiable view of human nature is to give unnecessary hostages to fortune. We certainly do not know enough confidently to assert or deny general propositions about the fixity or changeability of 'human nature'. Nor is new evidence likely to throw much light on this problem. What is politically controllable to a degree is not so much people's attitudes but their behaviour. One cannot easily change an attitude of contempt towards 'minority groups' but one can by legislation prevent the attitude exhibiting itself as discrimination. Of course it is true that people's attitudes change as they come, under the pressure of legislation, to change their behaviour. Attitudes to child labour, of course, have changed dramatically – in part due to reformist legislation in the nineteenth and twentieth century. Nevertheless it remains true that one cannot with any certainty predict that attitudinal change will flow from behavioural change.

Why not, it might be argued, try to change both attitude and behaviour at once and in harness? Why shouldn't propaganda be directed towards positive encouragement of cooperation and fraternity? Well, there may be nothing wrong in that – subject to one proviso. That being, that 'being a socialist' or 'having a conception of a socialist society' is not predicated upon having certain desirable attitudes! All a 'socialist' needs to demonstrate his political sincerity is a clear commitment to increasing freedom, and to enhancing equality. His lack of 'cooperativeness', personal altruism and courtesy are as irrelevant as his cigarette smoking or his love life.

The pursuit of freedom and equality are then the characteristically substantive features of socialism. But what of their relationship? Can one only be achieved at the expense of the other? In other words, is freedom inherently unfair?

It might appear so. As J.R. Lucas points out,[2]

If I have any liberty then there are some decisions I am allowed to make on my own; I am free in some cases to act arbitrarily. . . . I may choose Jane, and take her to wife, while passing over Bess her equally well-favoured sister. This is what it is to be free. . . . I may choose one person rather than another without there being any ground to justify discrimination.

Now it is certainly true that on some occasions the notion of acting upon whim or acting arbitrarily stands opposed to the notion of equality. To share out rewards or resources indiscriminately even if I may happen to distribute them in equal shares is inconsistent with the principle of equality. An egalitarian could not consistently say, 'Of course I happened to divide up the money equally but I might just as well have decided to give it all to Jane.' The freedom of the individual to act upon whim is, in this context, constrained by a rule which prima facie requires equality of distribution. Few people I imagine would urge the application of a rule of equality in the kind of case or cases Lucas cites. There is something unhealthily puritanical about individuals who require us to justify our person preference for one person over another in terms of high principle. These are areas of personal choice in which questions of equal treatment do not normally arise. I may prefer as friends the loquacious to the silent, the slim to the fat, the wit to the moralist but I may not choose to give reasons for so doing. If, however, amongst these categories of personal likes and dislikes I include 'skin colour' then what has been merely a question of personal whim is extended into the realm of the social. It is significant that there exists no socially defined group 'the loquacious' whereas there certainly is a social category based upon skin colour and in 'deciding' whether to discriminate on that basis one is involved in a social judgment in which one's freedom is limited morally speaking by a principle of equality of respect.

Conclusion: morality and socialism

Of course the line between the personal and the social is not all that hard and fast. To exclude fat people from one's circle of friends might well be construed as a social rather than a purely personal judgment. Everything hinges perhaps upon whether the excluded category is materially discriminated against in the wider society. Nevertheless, Lucas is in some sense right when he argues that freedom is inherently unfair. In personal matters, however, we often do not care about the unfairness of freedom. In social matters it is different. Here we may demand that freedom be sacrificed to fairness.

But speaking of 'freedom being sacrificed' still supports Lucas's way of presenting the problem – if freedom is unfair and we support what is fair then freedom goes by the board. On this argument every advance in equality diminishes freedom; every protection of freedom effectively hinders the promotion of equality.

This argument, unhappily for utopian socialists, has some limited force. In so far as I interfere with individual liberty to promote some other and distinct moral good I am sacrificing liberty. But the argument does not end there – indeed it has scarcely begun. What is vastly more illuminating is to consider the question of whether the pursuit of equality is necessarily incompatible with the extension of freedoms, for in denying liberty to some I may be enhancing the freedom of others. Lest this sounds dangerously totalitarian or close to reliance upon the 'positive' concept of freedom I have been at pains to criticise let me consider how inequalities may operate as constraints upon people's wishes. This procedure will be perfectly consistent with treating freedom as 'absence of constraint'.

Inequalities may be directly or indirectly constraining. Direct constraint may be exercised upon individuals by the deliberate and self-conscious pursuit of inegalitarian policies; indirect constraints may arise where human intentions or the unintended consequences of people's actions are mediated through what in metaphorical terms sociologists refer to as 'social structure'.

Consider a situation in which a government consciously decided to alter the system of taxation so as to favour the rich. Other things being equal the burden of taxation transferred to the poorer classes will clearly act as a constraint. Less money means less opportunity, more restrictions and additional burdens. Inegalitarian government policies will have directly led to a diminution of freedom.

On the other hand some government policies, perhaps even those intended to remedy inequalities, fail because of the indirect operation of 'the social structure'.

In spite of measures designed to give working class boys and girls greater educational opportunity it is still true that the children of upper and middle class families are strongly over-represented in most English universities. Why this is so is a complex question. The answer may relate to the interplay of the expectations of selectors, teachers, children and parents or to the 'different set of values' embraced by some working class parents. It is difficult to be sure here without running the risk of making a number of unexamined general assumptions about 'the working class' and its attitudes. Nevertheless it remains clear that working class access to elite forms of education is restricted not so much by direct policy but by the affects of a wide range of human decisions and attitudes none of which necessarily implies that particular result.

Of course many governments who deliberately pursue anti-egalitarian polices argue that their actions are justified since in the long term inequalities of reward and status increase efficiency and raise the standards of those lower in the hierarchy. If this argument can be sustained it defeats the egalitarian's contention that inequalities are a source of constraint. Compare the arguments:

   (a)   Egalitarian (E)
         (i) Poverty constrains

(ii) poverty is remediable through the abolition of inequalities

(iii) inequalities constrain

and

(b) Anti-Egalitarian (A)
(i) poverty constrains
(ii) the existence of 'appropriate' inequalities ameliorates poverty
(iii) inequalities of themselves do not necessarily constrain.

Whatever the validity of these arguments (E is of course formally invalid as it stands) it is demonstrably true that arguments both favouring or tending to deny the link between inequality and constraints upon what people want to do may depend upon economic theories of some complexity.

This, however, in no way undermines the egalitarian case since what is important is not argument derived from highly general and contentious economic theories but the empirically demonstrable existence of both poverty and inequality. Can it plausibly be asserted that taxation of the very rich to provide decent housing for those in need, for example, might actually damage the interests of the needy? Can it be maintained that the interests of the poor are systematically and typically enhanced by allowing economic freedom to the rich?

No amount of specious reference to 'incentives', 'trickle-down effects', 'reward for initiative' and so forth can convince me that the range of inequalities both in our society and others is justified in virtue of its supposed 'demonstrable' benefit to the poor. And surely such paradoxical statements as 'if you wish to improve the position of the poor allow free rein to the rich' stand in need of very compelling argument and empirical evidence when contrasted with the immediately perceptible constraining features of present inequalities.

Many right-wing economists of course will dismiss these comments as naive – evidence of a kind of primitive Robin Hood mentality. Yet democratic socialism owes more to Robin Hood than Karl Marx. The simple act of redistribution of wealth from the richer to the poorer classes does not seem to reduce the amount of wealth available for redistribution. Until it can be shown that egalitarian policies clearly diminish the position of the poor the prima facie case for egalitarianism remains undisturbed. Inequalities, then, constrain; the removal of inequalities enhances the (negative) freedom of those so constrained at the cost of diminishing the (negative) freedom of the privileged.

The proper questions to be raised in the pursuit of a just balance of the principles of liberty and equality are, then:

(i) Does the removal of a specified inequality promote the liberty of those who are in that respect unequal?

(ii) Does the removal of the specified inequality infringe upon the freedom of others? If so, upon whom and in what respect?

and (iii) Is the infringement of liberty in case (ii) justified or unjustified?

The questions are, of course, abstract but their answers must relate to particular circumstances.

Many political philosophers, however, have sought to produce theories at varying levels of generality which seek to reconcile equality with liberty. Some have argued for a high-level 'lexical ordering' of principles;[3] others have argued for a conception of justice in which no person should be dominant in one sphere of social life in virtue of his or her dominance in another.[4] On this latter 'pluralist' account of justice the priority of 'freedom' over 'equality' would be determined within relatively distinct 'spheres' of the human good, e.g.

security and welfare would be governed by 'need' whilst reward and punishment would be governed by 'desert'.

Such a conception, however, still leaves unanswered the question of how we are to decide when such relatively 'autonomous spheres' intersect or where there is genuine debate about the appropriateness of forwarding freedom of equality in a particular sphere. Should 'reward' (in itself a questionable notion) be necessarily linked with 'desert?'; should we promote or accept hierarchy in the workplace but not in our private lives?

I believe that there is no general answer to these questions. What underlies any proper conception of a just society are two monumental principles – those of 'freedom' and 'equality'. We appeal to the relevance of both in our moral deliberations but neither one nor the other compels us to a particular verdict. This distinction between 'deliberative' and 'verdictive' judgments is of the essence. In deliberations one establishes the relevance of first principles; in giving a verdict one makes a practical recommendation based upon particular applications of both or many principles simultaneously. Sometimes the verdict will enable us to have our cake and eat it; on other occasions the 'having' may take priority over the 'eating'. Socialism involves us in giving verdicts which are appropriate to diminishing burdens or, where they are inevitable, sharing them equally.

The failure to be able to specify some general relationship between equality and freedom which would assist us in coming to verdicts by a kind of 'rule of thumb' is not really a deficiency at all. Indeed 'mechanical' interpretation of clashes of principles in one or other direction would be a disaster. Nor does the failure to specify such a relationship result in irredeemable vagueness or obscurity. We may deduce from the application of the principles, for example, that civil liberties ought everywhere to be defended; that the public should have the widest possible access to information; and that hierarchy be everywhere opposed unless there appears compelling reason for its continuance; and so forth.

There is no easy move from seeing the relevance of a particular moral principle to determining whether it be granted overriding practical application to a particular moral policy or policies. Yet the establishment of the meaning and significance of general moral principles places the onus upon the critic to argue a special case for their not applying to a particular case. Socialists make a presumption in favour of freedom and equality; for contemporary theorists of the right such a presumption is denied. Whatever particular policies flow from these presumptive differences it is highly significant that the manner in which they are defended is determined by a very different set of moral presuppositions at the most general level.

The 'ultimate' justifications of presumptions in favour of or against freedom and equality are the very stuff of much moral philosophising. Perhaps, after all is said and done, the demand for 'ultimate' justifications is misplaced. This does not mean, however, that we have to abandon the possibility of moral rationality. Considerations may be adduced which influence our intellect as well as our sympathies to one set of values over another. If this were not so, moral argument would be pointless.

But surely, some critics would argue, all this high-flown moralising is beside the point on other grounds. Democratic socialism, it may be suggested, is politically impotent since it works within the 'rules of the game' which are set by its staunchest enemies – the capitalist class. While there may be a grain of truth in this contention it is wildly misleading. Democratic socialism is of course committed to political pluralism – to the possibility of its own periodic electoral defeat. In order to safeguard individual liberty and to avoid corruption and ossification it needs to encourage diversity of political opinion and action. From both the 'extreme' left and right such diversity is seen as inherently divisive. The social organism is viewed, as it were, as being predicated upon the possibility of a consensus on 'fundamental values'. If this consensus is not present, so it is argued, it needs to be imposed. This view is wholly misguided. It often functions as an apology for tyranny and oppression of minority opinion. What is necessary in a democratic society is the arbitration of substantive political conflict through a system of agreed procedures which cut across political party allegiance. What holds the democratic political process together is not 'value consensus' across the board nor the suppression of supposed 'socially dangerous' elements but agreement upon a range of arbitration measures sufficient to guarantee smooth political transitions where these are required by the electoral process. No doubt such existing procedures are not wholly neutral with respect to the exercise of political power but to represent them in principle as simply the 'ideological reflections' of a corrupt and corrupting mode of economic organisation is thereby to abandon the very possibility of both socialism and democracy.

Notes

Introduction
1 M. Cranston, *Freedom: A New Analysis*, London, Longmans, 1963.
2 J. Rawls, *A Theory of Justice*, Oxford University Press, 1971.
3 I. Gilmour, *Inside Right*, London, Quartet, 1978, Preface.
4 R. Scruton, *The Meaning of Conservatism*, London, Macmillan, 1980.
5 Ibid., p.19.

Chapter 1 The idea of freedom
1 For discussion of this see I. Berlin, *Four Essays on Liberty*, Oxford University Press, 1969, Introduction and Chapter 3.
2 C. Taylor, 'What's wrong with negative liberty?' in A. Ryan, *The Idea of Freedom*, Oxford University Press, 1979.
3 Ibid., p.177.
4 Ibid., p.180.
5 Ibid., p.180.
6 M. Friedman, *Capitalism and Freedom*, Chicago University Press, 1962.
7 Ibid., p.8.
8 Ibid., p.12.
9 Ibid., p.10.
10 Ibid., p.13.
11 G. Cohen, *Capitalism, Freedom and the Proletariat*, in A. Ryan, op. cit., pp.9–25.
12 J.S. Mill, 'On Liberty', in *Utilitarianism, Liberty and Representative Government*, London, J.M. Dent (Everyman), 1948.

13 Ibid., p.75.
14 Ibid., p.114.
15 National Executive Committee of the Labour Party, *Response to the National Front*, London, September 1978.
16 J.S. Mill, op. cit., p.149.
17 Ibid., pp. 72–3.
18 G. Dworkin, *Taking Rights Seriously*, Bristol, Duckworth, 1977.
19 R.J. Arneson, 'Mill versus paternalism', in *Ethics*, vol.90, no.4, July 80, University of Chicago Press, pp.470–89.

Chapter 2   Equality and fraternity
1 T. Honderich, *Three Essays on Political Violence*, Oxford, Blackwell, 1976.
2 S.I. Benn and R.S. Peters, *Social Principles and the Democratic State*, London, Allen & Unwin, 1959, Chapter 5.
3 Ibid., p.110.
4 J.D. Lucas, 'Against equality', in *Philosophy*, vol.40, no.154, October 1965, pp.296–307.
5 J. Rawls, *A Theory of Justice*, Oxford University Press, 1971.
6 Ibid., p.60.
7 Ibid., p.60.
8 T. Honderich, op. cit.
9 J. Rawls, op. cit., p.83.
10 K. Nielsen, *Impediments to Radical Egalitarianism*, in *American Philosophical Quarterly*, vol.18, no.2., April 1981, pp.121–9.
11 R. Nozick, *Anarchy, State and Utopia*, Oxford, Blackwell, 1974.
12 Ibid.
13 Ibid.
14 K. Nielsen, 'A Rationale for egalitarianism', in *Social Research*, vol.48, no.2, Summer 1980.
15 K. Nielsen, *Impediments to Radical Egalitarianism*, op. cit.
16 R. Dahrendorf, 'On the origins of social inequality', in P. Laslett and W.G. Runciman (eds), *Philosophy, Politics and Society*, Oxford University Press, 1962, pp.83–109.
17 S. Lukes, 'Socialism and equality', in L. Kolakowski and S. Hampshire (eds), *The Socialist Idea*, quoted in K. Nielsen,

Impediments to Egalitarianism, op. cit.

18 W.G. Runciman, *Relative Deprivation and Social Justice*, London, Routledge & Kegan Paul, 1966.

19 Ibid.

Chapter 3   Conclusion: morality and socialism

1 G. Orwell, *The Road to Wigan Pier*, London, Left Book Club, Victor Gollancz, 1937, p.248.

2 J.R. Lucas, 'Against equality', in *Philosophy*, vol.40, no.154, October 1964, pp.269–307.

3 J. Rawls, *A Theory of Justice*, Oxford University Press, 1971.

4 M. Walzer, *Spheres of Justice: A Defence of Pluralism and Equality*, Oxford, Martin Robinson, 1983.

Index

Index

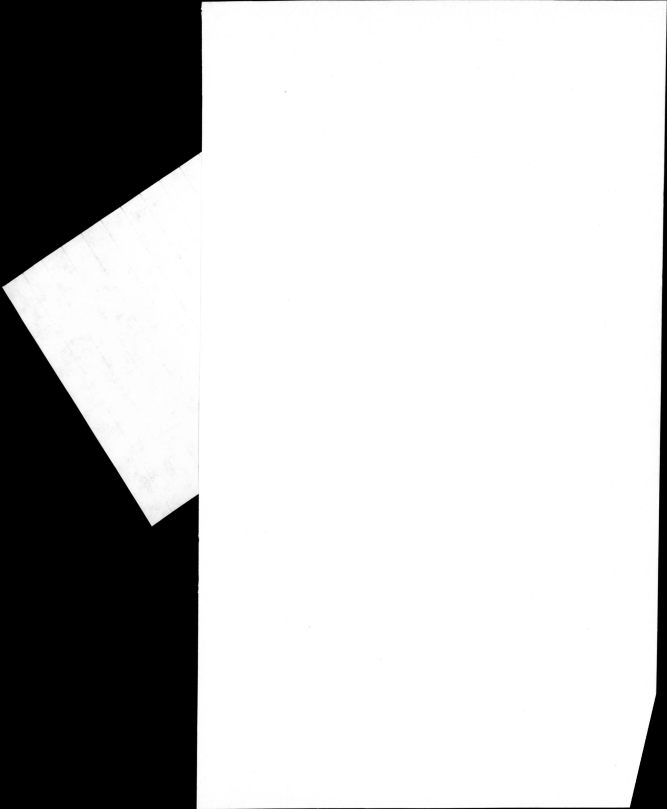

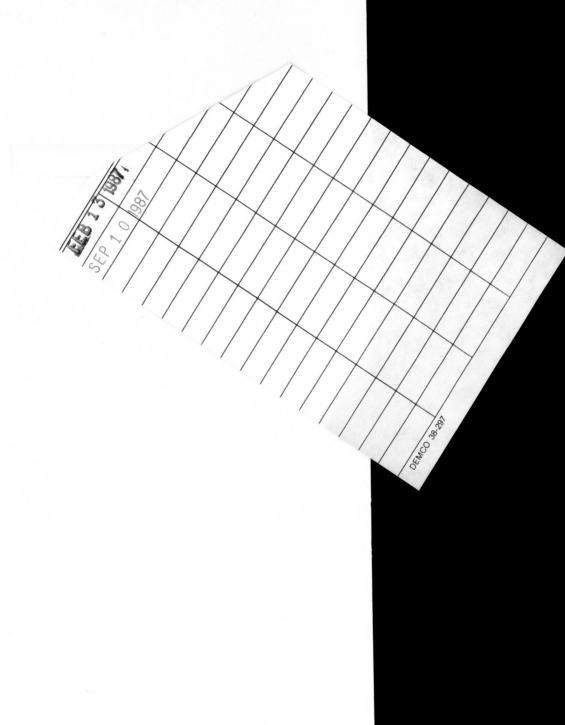